Shitty Bosses &
Asshole Employees

Shitty Bosses & Asshole Employees

Don't Read this Book!

CRYSTAL ISHIHARA, PH.D.
ISHIHUMANN INCORPORATED

This book is dedicated to the man who put up with my "writing juice" for a month of late nights, bleary-eyed conversation, and ignored Netflix time. Thanks for marrying me even after all of that. I do not deserve you.

And to the phoenix of a woman who has literally risen from the dead, you have my heart, my thanks, and I will NEVER forget everything you have done for me. You are an inspiration and my hero.

And last but not least, to the amazing duo that made me and raised me, I'm sorry for all of the swearing, but this is the time and the place. Thank you for letting me be myself, and loving me for it. You are magnanimous.

"The long and short of it: I. Loved. This.

It's insightful, useful, funny, and incredibly easy to relate to. The audience is distanced in the intro and then pulled into the fold in a unique and engaging way. I love the "tough love" approach; this book takes a hard, honest look at what people can do to change, what best practices and methods are, and what a toxic work environment looks like. Importantly, it refuses to let the reader bypass recognizing their own flaws and weak points, but it also doesn't make the reader feel alienated or judged for not being perfect. Gold nuggets of wisdom are liberally sprinkled throughout, and I wanted to scoop up every single one because 1) I really came to like and be engaged with the author's voice and persona and 2) I genuinely felt I was learning life lessons in a way that wasn't condescending, pretentious, or tedious. The 'personal story' touch followed by the psychological breakdown (with examples and questions, no less!) is a really awesome way to get the reader really thinking, processing, and engaged. This book creates space for the reader to feel "in it together" with the author and results in the reader doubling-down on the effort to understand and retain the message."

CONTENTS

FOREWORD
by Boulder

I've always known I would work for Crystal Ishihara. I knew it as soon as I met her. It's not that I'm psychic; she is just that good. I met Crystal when I was hired as a temp for an educational institution. She was a student worker for the same school. We were both working for the Registrar's office and within a few minutes of meeting her, I told her, "You're going to be my boss someday." She laughed, and we continued to joke about it, but I knew that it was going to come true. The thing is, the more I worked with her, the more I WANTED her to be my boss. Even though I am ten years older than she is, she surpasses me in every category you would want in a boss. Smart, check. Collaborative, double check. Leads by example, triple check.

I've had lots of bosses in my life. They usually fall into one of three categories:

1. Nice person to hang out with, but terrible at getting stuff done.
2. Gets stuff done but you don't ever want to see them outside of work.
3. Nice person, gets stuff done, but will never really excel in anything.

Crystal is in a category of her own.

She is a really kind and thoughtful person. She listens to people she works with and creates an environment where everyone feels comfortable working together to solve a problem. She gives credit where credit is due.

She's the smartest person in the room. Always. But, she never talks down to people or makes them feel stupid. She usually figures things out faster than other people but is also patient when it takes them some extra time to solve it themselves.

She's also very creative. Not only can she sing, craft a beautiful castle for a friend's daughter's birthday, or solve an escape room by herself, she wrote this book that you are reading. Plus, she suggested that I write the foreward. She's brilliant.

I hope writing this will count positively for my evaluation this year since Crystal is still my boss. And if anyone reading this book ever has the opportunity to work with or for Crystal Ishihara, you should jump at the chance.

She is just that good!

AN INTRODUCTION OF SORTS:
A Warning to Turn Back

Hi there. If you are reading this, you are probably looking for an answer of some sort. You are trying to figure out how you can be a better boss, or maybe just less of a terrible boss. More likely, you are looking for somebody to understand the way that you feel about your shitty boss. Maybe you are extremely fed up with the way you are treated at work. Maybe you think this book can provide a way to better deal with your current work situation. I'm here to tell you that it's not. This book is not an answer to anyone's problems, so let's get you to stop thinking that right up front. Apologies for whatever amount of time or resources you've wasted reading this paragraph, but hopefully you can cut your losses and move on with your awesome life. Go ahead, I won't judge you. I won't even know, trust me. To be honest, the rest of this introduction is going to try to discourage you from reading the rest of the book, so if I'm losing you, I'm actually doing my job.

For everyone else that is still here, let's talk about what this is about. When we get right down to it, the truth is that this book is about the annoying and frustrating crap I've had to deal with in my very long life. That's a joke by the way. My life, in the grand scheme of things, has not been that long if you compare it to other folks who have written books like this. As I sit here about to spew a ton of knowledge and wisdom out to the world, I am the "antique" age of 33. That was sarcasm, obviously....Did I lose anyone else? That's fine. I'm writing this for the people who are at a similar point in their lives. This is for those of us not quite fresh out of college and have been working for a while, but maybe don't have a "seat at the table" just yet. (If you don't fit into that category and want to keep reading, I won't stop you.).

If you had to peg me into a certain age group, I guess I'm an aging millennial. I grew up before the internet was widespread, and I didn't get a cellphone (cell, for you hipsters) until I was just about to graduate from high school. I know what a floppy disk is also known as "the 3D print-out of the save button" (jeez), and I remember when my mom used to play vinyl records on the stereo. But I'm not, by any means, someone who doesn't buy into the idea that recycling is good, or that humans are terrible, or that beards are sexy...okay, maybe a little too personal there. Hopefully, that gives you an idea of the perspective I'm coming from. I feel like it's one that is sorely lacking right now. There are a ton of articles about millennials in the workforce, but there aren't a ton written by millennials. So in true nerd form, I am hoping to contribute to the existing literature with a book that is chock full of anecdotal stories about working, bosses, and hopefully, some insight from someone who's still speaking from the millennial perspective, aging though I may be.

You're probably wondering what qualifies me to write this book. I did some digging, and there are not many qualifications needed to sit down and write a book.

- **You need to have a grasp of some language.** I'm choosing English because, even though I'm Asian-American, English is the only language I am fluent in.
- **You need a topic you want to talk about or some story to tell.** I chose shitty bosses because I've had many, and I truly enjoy saying horrible things about them, thus fulfilling both the topic and story markers. Yes, I get that may make me an asshole, and I'm perfectly fine with that.
- The only other thing (and to be fair, this is the biggest deal), is that I think you need to have **some kind of persistence** hidden away somewhere to fuel the potentially futile attempt to produce something out of nothing but the thoughts in your head.

That is what I think it takes to write a book. And this, folks, is my attempt to figure out if I actually have those qualifications. Good luck sticking around for the ride and I apologize in advance for what is to come.

Let's talk about the actual qualifications I have, and maybe you'll think they warrant my perspective. For starters, I've been working since I was 16 years old which and if you've done the math (like my editor did), that's over half of my life! These years of employment gave me some pretty good perspective on what a shitty boss looks like since most of my bosses have been just terrible. I've worked in a few different industries starting at an ice cream shop, retail, retail management, head-hunting, and finally ended up in academia. But I'm still figuring out what I want to be when I grow up. I do my best not to hop from job to job, and I usually stick around for about three years before something catastrophic happens that makes me want to leave a job. With that said, I don't think I'm entirely unreasonable or unrealistic.

I've also gone to school for a really, really long time, some of it while I've been working. I double majored in Psychology and Advertising in my undergraduate years, earned my Master of Arts in Industrial/Organizational Psychology, and *finally* got my Doctor of Philosophy in Business Psychology. If you don't already know what Industrial/Organizational Psychology and Business Psychology are about, they are basically the study of people at work. My terrible bosses propelled me into a field where I wanted to study people at work and figure out how to:

1. make their lives less shitty by
2. fixing their bosses or
3. helping them to learn how to deal with their terrible bosses.

Hopefully, you have a little more faith in me now that you know I'm a doctor. Maybe my dissertation will give you some additional confidence? Mine was about how conflict management styles affect the potential for burnout. If you're reading between the lines, I was trying to figure out how relationships (mostly with your bosses) can have an effect on burnout which usually results in people quitting their jobs. Predictable, I know.

As it turns out, I have also been and am currently a boss. And I don't mean like those people that post Facebook memes saying they are a "boss at life," or a "boss bitch," or whatever. I mean that I have actual subordinates who I work alongside every Monday through Friday except (of course) holidays and vacations. They are some of my favorite people in the world, and I respect them for putting up with me. One of them was even kind enough to write the foreword. And no, he didn't get any compensation for that because, well, it's above my pay grade. The academic world simply doesn't work that way. He was pretty excited to write it for some weird reason, though. My team and I have been working together for over two years and, to be honest, the only reason I am their boss is because they asked me to take the promotion. I am forever thankful for everything that they do because I know that they work their asses off.

All right, so I've worked a lot, I'm pretty realistic, I've studied this stuff for a really long time, and I've got some experience being a boss. Those are my qualifications for now.

You are probably wondering how this book is actually going to play out. If everything goes right I am going to spend each chapter talking about a boss that I've had who has made some kind of impact on me. Usually, this means they were either really shitty or really awesome. Yes, I've got some chapters about what to do right because I think those wonderful people deserve a lot of credit, and I appreciate having had them at some point in my professional career.

In the chapters about the terrible bosses I've survived, I'll tell you what they did and why it frustrated me. The goal is to give you a window into my perspective in the hopes that it gives you some insight into your own situation or helps you consider your employees. At the end of the book, I have a long checklist that explains "how to be a good boss."

This whole book will boil down to two things: respect and transparency. If you don't have time to read all of this (because really, who has any time today?), being a good boss is about honesty and treating employees the way that you want to be treated. Is your team tasked with a major project that is extremely tedious that no one wants to do? If you were in your employees' situation, wouldn't you sincerely appreciate your boss's offer to help out? If the answer is yes, then chip in. If you think the answer is no, then you are either kidding yourself, or they do not respect your offer to help – and both are major problems. If you can't chip in because you need to work on more pressing matters, be honest and let your team know; they will understand. Give them the benefit of being mature enough to understand your position, and they will appreciate you for it. We're getting a little too much into the "meat" of the book, so let's discuss an overview, shall we?

What you can expect:

- *An Ice Cream Shop, a Teenager, and a Shitty Boss:* Dealing with Change Management, Fairness, and Perceived Competence
- *Music is the Road to My Soul, and Chuck Norris is the Best Boss Ever:* Helping Employees to Succeed Through Coaching and Training
- *When the Music Dies and Scarface is Not a Movie:* Ignoring Liars and Being Asshole Employees
- *Retail Napoleon:* Keeping Your Ego Out of the Equation
- *The Good, the Bad, and the Learning Curve:* A Case for Cross-Training, Succession Planning, and Delegation
- *Everything You Ever Wanted, Even for a Moment:* Supporting Employees Who Show Promise

- **Spineless and Ridiculous:** What Happens When You Don't Respect Your Employees
- **Director Idol:** The Boss That You Want to Be

I think that's it. Are you ready to be entertained by witty stories about shitty bosses? Let's hope not because I am not even going to promise you that. Two caveats: Obviously all of their names have been changed. I'm also writing about some experiences that happened over a decade ago so please forgive any liberties I take along the way. I'll leave one final warning to anyone still reading this: TURN BACK. Do not pass GO. You do not have to keep reading this piece of...

Still here? Okay, well here goes nothing.

CHAPTER 1:
An Ice Cream Shop, a Teenager, and a Shitty Boss

For my sanity, I've decided to write this in near chronological order. As a 16-year-old my very first job was working at a local ice cream shop. For the sake of anonymity, we'll call it TICS (The Ice Cream Shop). Yes, I know, super inventive and witty. I grew up in a family where you had to figure out how to get what you wanted on your own. If it wasn't food, clothing, or school-related, just imagine your parents shaking their heads and maybe even making you feel guilty for asking, it's what parents do. This is especially true when you are the oldest of four kids and start asking for a drum set of all things. Go ahead and laugh, but that's what this pseudo punk rock, emo-kid had her heart set on. Playing the saxophone in the high school marching band was not fulfilling the "darkness" in my soul, and I desperately wanted to start a band and create my own music. I knew the only way to get my hands on a set of my own was to get a job, save up, and buy it. Oh, my poor little goth heart was insatiable.

Fortunately for me, my mom was friendly with the owner at TICS. She got me a job with no résumé and a fifteen-minute interview which consisted of me somehow convincing the manager that, even though I had no experience, I was willing to work hard, be on time, and learn as quickly as I could. My very first boss got me to promise to smile more because that was the only way to get customers to put extra cash in the tip jar next to the register. I was elated - one step closer to getting that drum set. I still didn't know how to play, but I had already it picked out at a shop downtown. High-school-me was unstoppable, and I'm pretty sure I carried around a pair of drumsticks to "practice" and give myself the constant reminder that working at TICS would be worth it.

Let's fast forward a little bit because the reality is that working at an ice cream shop is a pretty sweet first gig (pun intended). Sure, you smell like chocolate ice cream when you get home from work at 11 o'clock at night, and your dad has to pick you up because you can't even drive yet, but other than that, it was pretty awesome for a teenager. Even though it made me an ice cream snob, I would definitely still work at another ice cream shop because the smell is damn intoxicating.

All was going well until the owner sold the shop back to the franchise owner, and I quickly learned what happens when a company changes management. Everything you've spent the past couple of months learning was "fine," but you now had to learn it a new and different way so that you could do things "better." To this day, I don't understand what was better about the new way, just that it was coming from a new manager who needed things to be done the way she wanted. By this time, I had been there long enough to be liked by the veteran employees who had worked at TICS for years. They taught me the best way to do things based on their experience and even helped me to up my customer service game. The previous owner had been right - if you don't smile, you are not going to get tips. I figured that out pretty quickly and to this day, I still unconsciously work for nonexistent tips. I liked my job. I was good at it, and the perks were awesome: free ice cream (if you messed up someone's order), being the lucky bastard who got to try every single ice cream flavor, AND make up all kinds of delicious sundae and milkshake concoctions. When the new owner came in, however, a lot of the best parts of the job went away.

For anonymity sake, we're going to call my boss Alice. Back when Alice started, I really didn't have any idea what it meant to be managed. My experience had only been reporting to the previous owner, but she didn't really manage any of the employees. Everyone had been there so long, they just knew what to do. I learned on the job and shadowed employees who had been around a little longer, but I was never put through a formal training process. It was pretty organic and I liked it. When Alice started she was friendly enough, and the other employees and I did our best to get her up to speed on how the shop ran. She was quick to ask questions and even quicker to point out the things we could do better. I hadn't been there long enough to be offended, but she definitely pissed off the other employees especially when her idea of "better" seemed to be more of a preference as opposed to actual improvement. They soon stopped wanting to work during the same shifts as her which meant I had the wonderful "opportunity" to work with her.

Alice wasn't a terrible person. She was extremely diligent and hardworking at times but also oddly lazy and irresponsible at others. To be fair, I think this is true of most employees. Most of us have certain parts of our job that we really enjoy doing, and we will go above and beyond expectations because it's something that we simply like to do. If it's a part of a job that we hate, we'll procrastinate or delegate it away. The problem with Alice was that she was the manager, and she didn't enjoy doing any of the managerial aspects of her job. Sure, she liked scooping ice cream and being friendly with customers and was even good at it. It was apparent she had never managed anyone before, and try as she might, she couldn't quite figure out how to do it in a way that worked for her and the employees.

When you are managing a small shop like TICS, there are certain things that must get done on time to keep the business running. Generally, there must be some product or service you are selling as well as the people who sell your product or provide your service. In an ice cream shop, it's pretty simple - you need to have ice cream in the store ready to sell, and you need to have employees to serve the ice cream to customers. Alice could not, for the life of her, figure out how to place an accurate ice cream supply order. She would over-order ice cream flavors that she liked and under order flavors that were top sellers. Our shop was located in Hawaii, and we tended to have a lot of abnormal flavors including the most popular flavor, Green Tea. It was camouflage green and looked kind of gross, but it was delicious. Alice hated Green Tea ice cream, and likely for that reason, she never ordered enough of it. In my teenage mind, I remember thinking it would have been pretty easy to figure out how much of each flavor we should order. We just had to keep track of the flavors ordered, the quantity needed for a full week, and use that to figure out the supply order for the rest of the month. I remember offering up that tiny gem of advice, but I was told that it wasn't that simple and that I should leave the ordering to Alice. I distinctly remember shortly after that conversation we ran out of Green Tea ice cream. Alice had to drive herself to the factory to pick up some extra supply to keep our customers happy. I'm annoyed all over again just thinking about it because that was the pattern every time we ran out of a popular flavor. Alice would have to drive to the factory, pay full price for the ice cream, and bring it back to the shop. If Alice wasn't working that day, we were basically out of luck and had to deal with annoyed customers for the rest of the shift. Maybe that doesn't seem like a multi-million dollar issue, but remind yourself how annoyed you are the next time you go to pick up something that is advertised, and it's not available. It's a simple problem that has an equally simple solution. If only Alice would have listened.

Let's get back to what it takes to run a small business. We've already discussed supply, so let's talk about the employees who provide a service or sell the product. At TICS we did both. We were tasked with convincing customers that an extra scoop was only $0.75 more, and then had to scoop the ice cream to make a sundae, shake, waffle cone, smoothie, or an ice cream cake. We were paid minimum wage to do it which was no problem on our end; we all knew what we had signed up for. The problem was that Alice could not put together a schedule that was perceived as fair or covered the length of store hours. She really didn't need to reinvent the wheel, as we had been running a pretty tight schedule for a while. It made sense for the current employees, and I don't really think that anyone had a problem with it. Alice could have easily copied the original schedule and made minor tweaks here and there. Unfortunately, she decided to disregard the current schedule to make a "better" one on her own. If you've never worked at a company where you rely on small shifts of people to come in and run your business, I imagine it's like trying to drive across America without stopping to rest. You always need someone to be awake enough to drive, and you really shouldn't make one person take on the entire load. You also shouldn't give the kid who just got there license the wheel for the majority of the time. Just saying.

Alice thought she could improve the schedule by equally dividing up the shifts instead of awarding the more favorable shifts to employees who deserved them (based on experience and work quality). This quickly upset the employees who had been there for a while as well as some of the overworked employees who weren't used to the increased load. When this happened, I was still in high school and quickly went from working two or three days a week to working four or five days a week. Let's just say that I'm lucky my high school teachers thought I was too smart to kick out of school because I slept through a lot of my Trigonometry and English classes *(To those teachers, I really am sorry, I was just trying to buy myself a drum set. Thank you for not docking my participation points)*. In retrospect, this routine of working way too many hours while going to school probably set me up for long-term success, but I wouldn't wish it on the average teenager who wants to have a social life. Mine quickly disappeared, that's for sure.

Alice never seemed to receive any kind of training to make supply orders or build a schedule. No one gave her the guidance to manage, and she was probably doing the best she could. I understand that a lot of companies don't really have great onboarding procedures or mentor-type programs that support a manager's professional development. That being said, Alice definitely had a chip on her shoulder. The reality is that while no one had shown Alice how to do her job, no one forced her to redo what had already been working well. Before Alice became the manager, we had an employee who handled the supply orders and would always be accurate with what was needed. If anything, she would over order a couple of cartons, but nothing that couldn't sell quickly enough. Alice could have easily continued to let that employee handle supply orders. We also had a schedule that worked, and she easily could have plugged herself into it and made minor changes as she saw fit. Like many managers, Alice was an Icarus flying too close to the "My Way or the Highway"-sun, and all of the ice cream melted along with her.

So, what did Alice do wrong?

Some of you may be getting a little defensive right about now because you are thinking that some companies need change to happen quickly but don't allow for much integration. That's a fair point, and I'm not saying that you're wrong. What I am saying is that maybe you can use this story to temper your perspective on how your change might affect the veteran employees who have worked for said company. When you make significant changes in a short amount of time without much explanation or logical improvements, you aren't doing yourself or your employees any favors.

When you make significant changes, you are increasing the potential for all aspects of burnout. Burnout is what occurs when an employee is emotionally exhausted, meaning that they have invested so much of their emotional energy into their job that they are entirely spent. They are figuratively too drained to care. Employees who are burned out depersonalize themselves from their job, meaning that they try to put distance between their sense of worth and the work that they do. While some employees may feel value due to their work, a burned-out employee can no longer derive that same feeling. They are no longer proud of their company and sometimes, unfortunately, themselves. This is likely because burnout also is reflected in an employee's feeling of low personal achievement because they don't think that they have any control or the ability to succeed. Altogether, this makes it easier for employees to become unhappy and eventually decide to leave your organization.

Dealing with change that is perceived as unnecessary can be emotionally taxing. Not only does an individual have to learn and adapt to the new way of doing things, but they also deal with the concept that the way they used to complete tasks was incorrect or ineffective. Unconsciously, that can have negative effects on an employee's sense of self-worth and, consciously, they will likely appear to be frustrated and may even act out. Depersonalization is when an employee begins to distance themselves from their job. Where they once might have been enthusiastic and motivated to be a high achiever, they may now be cynical or use sarcasm in response to general requests. Trust me on the sarcasm part; it has always been my go-to reaction when I am annoyed at something. The last bit of burnout is the loss of feelings of personal achievement or efficacy, which basically means that your employees start to feel like they aren't making a difference. This doesn't mean that your employees previously thought that they were going to change the world. Scooping ice cream is great and all, but it's definitely not going to solve world hunger. From my perspective, when an employee starts feeling they are no longer effective or achieving at their job, they start to question why they are even there. Remember how I had started working at TICS to buy myself a drum set? By the time Alice showed up and made all of her changes, I was ready to give up my rock star mentality just so I wouldn't have to deal with her anymore. When an employee starts to look for a way out, you have to consider that you're doing something wrong. When most of your employees decide they would rather be unemployed than work for you, then you KNOW you're doing something wrong. In a nutshell, when you don't manage change appropriately, you are potentially causing your employees to burnout and likely pissing them off them while doing it.

There are a lot of ways that change management has been discussed, and this book isn't really about addressing the best ways of doing that so I won't pretend to be an expert on it. What I will talk about are a couple of ways that Alice could have handled the changes she wanted to make in a way that made sense for TICS employees.

First of all, Alice always had some new and improved idea about how to do something we were already doing pretty well. Redoing the schedule is a great example of that: she became our manager and, without much explanation, quickly decided the schedule wasn't right and that it needed to change. We were not given a chance to provide any input. We weren't asked why the schedule was set up the way it was. We were simply told the schedule was going to change and that we needed to provide our availability. I'm going to give Alice the benefit of the doubt and say that she wanted to spread shifts out in what she perceived to be a more equitable way instead of giving a majority of the shifts to the "old-timers." As a manager myself some years later, I had a similar thought. The reality though is that not every employee wants an equal distribution of shifts.

For example, when I was asked to provide my availability, I indicated that I was able to work every day from 3:00 pm to close (i.e. 8 hour shifts) and all day during the weekends (i.e. 13 hours per day, opening at 10:00 am and closing at 11:00 pm). Did that mean I actually wanted to work that many hours? Absolutely not! For those of you that like to do math, that would have meant I would have worked eight hours daily during the week (totaling 40 hours) and 26 additional hours over the weekend if they allowed overtime. I wasn't trying to work 66 hours a week! I was in high school, didn't have a car, or even know how to drive yet. Getting to work was a burden unto itself back then, and I didn't need to pay rent or anything. Other employees worked multiple jobs because they actually *had* to pay their rent. While their availability might have been limited, they became accustomed to working the days indicated on their availability. The previous owner used to create the schedule based on employee experience and quality of service. She gave the busy shifts to the old-timers who were available and could handle the inevitable rush of customers after dinner, and then she filled in the additional shifts with the new employees who often had more availability. This made sense on a couple of levels because it respected seniority and experience while making sure that shifts were covered. Alice didn't exactly see the schedule that way. It seemed like she took the availability everyone provided and gave them half of the shifts they had listed. She may have thought it was fair, but the more experienced employees felt disrespected, and the newer employees were left to scramble to cover their shifts.

So, what should Alice have done differently?
I don't think I've made it a secret that she should have enlisted our help. It helps to get the lay of the land when you start a new position. Understand what has worked and where improvement is needed and ask a lot of questions. Don't barrel into a situation "guns blazing" thinking you're going to save the world with your great schedule-changing idea. The reality is that there is likely already a process in place if you are stepping into an existing position. You would be silly to think the issue you are trying to solve hasn't already been addressed in some way or that existing

employees haven't already mulled over how to improve it. Don't get me wrong, there will be plenty of times where you recognize a gap that needs to be filled. But you've got a wealth of knowledge in the employees that have been living the "problem" you are trying to solve, and they should be the first people you consult for ideas on how to make improvements. Maybe they don't have any ideas how to fix it, but don't assume that right off the bat. By doing so, you're disrespecting their intelligence and their experience. You're also likely wasting a lot of time, especially if they've already tried out the solution you are proposing. Bottom line: ask questions first, shoot later.

In Alice's case, she was a nice manager. She didn't yell or scream at any of us, and she definitely didn't create a hostile work environment or anything as intense as that. She did, however, have an inexplicably large ego. This is a personal pet peeve of mine. As humans we are all fallible and prone to doing very stupid things. For as long as I can remember, I have done at least one completely idiotic thing every day of my life, including the day I earned my Ph.D. We're a very VERY stupid species. Most other species have to fend for themselves right out of the womb. Can you imagine a baby human trying to figure out how to take care of themselves that early on? As a very dumb species, the amount of people with ridiculously large egos makes no sense to me. It also seems to negatively correlate with their actual level of intelligence; i.e., the dumber you are, the bigger your ego. Anyway... moving off of that tangent.

Alice came from the perspective that she knew how to do everything better than the rest of us, even though she had never worked in our shop and had never managed anyone before. She didn't like to ask for our help and refused any advice given to her. It didn't matter that her ideas didn't actually end up working most of the time. Evidence of her failed ideas just meant that we weren't doing things the right way. Oh Alice, I hope you have since learned that you are not as smart as you think you are.

My suggestion here is a pretty simple one. Repeat after me: I am not the smartest person in the room. For the folks who need to give speeches and have to picture the audience naked or whatever, please disregard the previous statement. For everyone else, say it one more time: I am not the smartest person in the room. It has been my personal experience that thinking I am the smartest person in any situation automatically disqualifies me from being so. A smart person knows that there is always something else to learn and someone to learn from. Do I have senseless amounts of fake ego to help convince myself I'm good enough to have a seat at the table? Yes, absolutely. But do I ever think for a second that I can't learn anything from anyone else? Of course not. Everyone has something to teach you, and when you find someone who believes they have nothing to share, you should learn some humility from them.

To recap, you don't have to yell at people to be a terrible boss, but you do have to respect them to make steps towards being a good one. Let your actions will speak louder than your words. Cliché? Yes. True? Also a resounding yes. Did Alice every call us idiots? No, not to our faces at least. She did however put a lot of effort into making it very clear to us that our opinions were not valued or helpful. The actions she took to disregard our perspective were just as harmful.

It's also important to keep your ego in check. People can tell when you think that you are better than them, and if they don't agree with your perspective, they are not going to respect or trust you. And your ego will not get you anywhere with your employees. You can use your ego to push through some of the noise in an overly pompous board meeting, but with your employees - the people who are actually doing the grunt work - your ego makes you look like an asshole, and nobody wants to work for an asshole. Ask for help and be overly appreciative of the help you receive. Pay respect to the years that your employees have put into their jobs and let them know that you couldn't do this job without them. And believe it, genuinely believe that your employees are the people who are holding you up, because if you treat them like they are, then they will.

Alice could have done many things differently and, without going further into annoying stories about what she did wrong, I'll give you a breakdown of some of the really easy things she could have done better.

When you are in charge of a small group, the likelihood of one of those people having an emergency or taking a vacation is pretty high. Then what happens? If you're in charge, you can't just let that person's tasks and responsibilities go undone. When you start working with a small team, one thing I have found to be helpful is learning how to be an understudy for your employees. If you already know how to fill in seamlessly, you (1) don't have that deer-in-the-headlights moment of panic, and (2) you look like a hero. It's important to figure out when and how to help as soon as possible, so you are well prepared if and when your help is needed.

You get further brownie points if you've got a team that is cross-trained to fill in for each other (so the workload is shared instead of all on you to manage). Seems simple on the face of it right? It's not, and I can appreciate that. I've always been promoted into higher-level positions (instead of hired into them), so I've always had the fortune of already knowing how to handle the responsibilities of the people working for me because I've literally done it before. If I hadn't been promoted up and was stepping into a new position, I can imagine it would be difficult to learn both my role and the role(s) of my team. The main point is that taking this piece of advice will be difficult, no doubt about it, but it will also be worth it. When your team feels like you understand their responsibilities, not only can you fill in at a moment's notice, but you are also working to earn the respect of your team. You learn where they are coming from, you understand how frustrated they are with certain issues, and you will then inevitably work together to naturally make improvements. This is killing five birds with one massive stone. More brownie points if you document your processes along the way. Standard Operating Procedures are life-saving when you can't remember that one extra step. You don't do these processes on a daily basis, and you are bound to forget, so WRITE THAT SHIT DOWN!!!!!

Another piece of advice and this one is easy - pay attention to what is important to your employees. If you've spent time understanding their jobs, you'll know what's important to them. Once you know, make sure you take special care to do your part and make sure it runs smoothly. In Alice's situation, the one thing that drove everyone absolutely crazy was when the schedule was late. Not only was the schedule a pain point because of its contents but when it was late, no one had any idea of what their personal life was going to be. If you work in a shift environment, do your best to make the schedule for at least a month in advance so that people can plan out their lives, they will love you for this. Alice put out a weekly schedule, often a day late, which meant we had to guess what our shifts would be for the week. As you can imagine that is extremely irritating for some college students and a high school kid (and her parents). She would spend her time working on store signs and new types of products we could sell when all anyone really wanted was the schedule. Go for the easy wins. If you step into a team that likes to leave a little early on Fridays to get drinks together, don't be the shithead new boss who makes them all stay 'till 5:00 pm for no reason, as long as it doesn't negatively impact the company. When the team you step into is already running well, make the effort to figure out why and retain what works. Change for the purpose of change is a waste of time and can drive hardworking employees crazy.

One last piece of advice for you, if you feel you're in a similar situation. I'm pretty sure I've already mentioned this somewhere, but two words: CHIP IN! Staying late to work with your team, taking your fair share of a tedious project, answering the customer service line, or taking out the trash: just do it. You are not too important that you can't afford to help out. And if you are that important, be honest and transparent about it. You don't have to help every single time, but as long as you do it when it counts your team will understand that you do not consider yourself above them. You are there to work together, you're just somehow the unlucky jerk that has to be in charge. You're showing them respect and you're also showing them that you deserve their respect. This tactic has worked from retail to academia. When people realize you are willing to help out they are that much more willing to go the extra mile for you.

So...what?: Survival Skills

This is all well and good for you if you're currently a terrible boss, and this story sounds a little too familiar to you. However, you are most likely reading this because you have a boss like Alice and are either burned out, on the verge of burning out, or are ready to put in your resignation letter. We're going to refer to this section as Survival Skills moving forward because while you may not enjoy the challenges your boss is putting you through, you can most likely put up with it (at the very least). I don't have a perfect formula, and I'm not going to pretend this part of the job is fun, but I'm happy to share with you what I did to get by.

First things first - when you realize your boss has an ego that doesn't necessarily match her qualifications (aka Alice), the easiest thing to do is to talk a lot of crap about them behind their back or defy them outright by calling them out when they mess something up. Sure, that will make you feel good for a short amount of time, and you'll be able to feed your own ego. But then what? You've managed to make your boss feel threatened and insecure. When you make people feel threatened or insecure, the last thing they want to do is trust you. Unfortunately, when dealing with your boss, one of your best tools is the ability to earn their trust and use it to your advantage. While my coworkers were quick to voice their frustrations, I was lucky enough not to have that many, so I let them air out their grievances without adding to the fray. This caused Alice to distrust my coworkers, which inadvertently made me the most likable and trustworthy of her employees. I'll admit I dumb-lucked myself into that situation, but it worked. There will be times when ethically you should voice your concerns, and we'll talk about that later. If your concerns are based on your personal preferences or desire to avoid change, it's helpful to get the full picture of a situation first.

I was lucky, I didn't really know any better, so I didn't have a lot to complain about. Since I was the last employee to figure out that Alice was a pain in the ass, I was pretty understanding and nice to her in the meantime. This can be aggravating as hell, especially if you are quick to realize that your boss sucks. What I suggest is giving your boss some time to try and navigate themselves into their new position.

In the same way that I think new bosses should get the lay of the land before they make huge changes, I also suggest that employees who work with new bosses give them the benefit of the doubt before they pass judgment. Give them a mental probation period and be helpful during that time. You can earn their trust, and then they will be that much more likely to hear you out when you have a suggestion. Figure out where they could use a little help and in a non-threatening way. Instead of saying "That's not how we do things around here" (or whatever your equivalent would be), say something like "What if we did it this way?" or "What if I show you how we do X task currently and get your input on how to improve it?" Being non-threatening and helpful to a new boss can go a long way towards building a positive working relationship. I get it...it may feel unfair that you have to do extra work to help your new boss, but you're really helping yourself in the long run.

When I realized Alice was doing a terrible job and would continue to do so, I switched gears ever so slightly. By the time I realized it, many of the employees who had been there a while either already found new jobs or were actively searching. In a short amount of time, I became one of the most trusted and experienced employees (serious shocker to my teenage self), and when I knew Alice was never going to do a good job, I took the initiative to put myself in a position to step into her role should it ever become vacant. I leveraged her trust in me to learn everything I could about how to do her job: closing the registers at the end of the night, offering to be an extra pair of eyes on supply orders, and eventually helping to build the schedule. I learned everything I could, and I would encourage you to do the same since it's both practical and strategic. From a practical standpoint, if your boss ever is no longer your boss, you know how to manage without her. From a strategic standpoint, if you are able to show that you can manage without your boss, you make yourself look much more attractive to become the next successor. I'd like to tell you this is what happened at TICS, but I found another job that paid more and left before Alice did. She was eventually "let go," and the shop owner was scrambling for a little while. Too bad about that non-existent contingency plan.

Another thing I did while learning about different managerial responsibilities was to improve my relationships with remaining employees and the new ones hired to deal with the turnover. My coworkers soon looked to me as a resource for process and random questions. Most of my coworkers considered my responses to be more accurate and timely than Alice's. I wasn't their boss, but I had become their unofficial leader. Unofficial leaders are the unsung heroes in the workplace. These are the folks who don't get paid to take care of teams of employees but do anyway. They are the people you turn to when you want to ask a "stupid question" or need to be reminded of how something works. An unofficial leader's perspective can often be more connected to the needs and wants of the employees, and they are usually a persuasive voice in the face of significant change. Sometimes, if you're lucky, unofficial leaders become official leaders, and they get the titles that go along with the work they've already been doing.

Dealing with an Alice as a boss sucked. The strategies I've described are not cure-alls, and they may not make any positive change for a while. Everyone's situation is different. You've tried something similar, and it bombed: That's fine. As I said earlier, the point of this book is not to solve your problems, but if nothing else, if you have to deal with an Alice, I hope you get the feeling that I understand a little about what you're going through. I fully get how fucking infuriated you are because I know that I was. I won't promise it will get better, but I would bet that you'll get through it. Best of luck, dude.

Ask yourself...do you feel lucky?

To close out this chapter, I'm going to leave a couple of questions here for you to consider. You don't have to write down your answers or turn this in as a class assignment - just some stuff for you to think about. It's broken up into two sections: Shitty Boss and Asshole Employee. If you're reading this, you're one of these people. There are two perspectives to every situation and as unbiased or reasonable as you think you might be, you will never fully understand how you are making someone else's life difficult. So, let's figure out which role you play, and how.

Shitty Boss:

1) While going through the chapter, specifically during the "So what did Alice do wrong?" section, did you bristle at certain topics and get defensive? If so, you might be a Shitty Boss.
   a. Think about it. Why did you get defensive? Is your argument legitimate, or are you spewing off an angry explanation to no one in particular right now because the circumstances "warranted your actions"?
   b. Everyone can be a Shitty Boss at times, just use this as a point of reflection so that you don't continue to be one. Don't let these moments define you.
2) Now that you've realized you're a Shitty Boss be honest with yourself and consider what you can do to improve. I said to be honest, so there's got to be something...I'll wait.
3) Once you've settled on something, how will you actually improve? Map out a plan and do it!!! Do it now. Your employees are waiting.

Asshole Employee:

1) While going through this chapter, did you relate to my frustrations with Alice? Why?
2) After considering your frustrations, can you explain what you did to alleviate them?
   a. Yes, I am asking what you did because there was likely something you could have done. If you didn't do anything that contributed to improvement, you aren't helping yourself.
   b. If you did something to alleviate the strain, did it work? Why or why not?
3) Now, think of something else that you can do, and do it.

The next chapter is a bit of a reprieve from our Shitty Boss story. You'll get to read about Chuck Norris, and what it's like to work at a record store. Spoiler alert - it's awesome!!

CHAPTER 2:
Music is the Road to My Soul, and Chuck Norris is the Best Boss Ever

I lied, sorry. Chuck Norris isn't the best boss ever. Or...well...maybe he is. I've never met him, so I can't confirm the title of this chapter to be true. Honestly, with the plethora of his accolades, I wouldn't doubt that the real Chuck Norris is actually the best boss ever. I mean, if the man doesn't do push-ups but in fact pushes the world down, I can imagine that he would have a pretty good idea of how to be an awesome boss. Damn, now I really want to meet Chuck Norris.

If I'm not talking about the real Chuck Norris, you're probably wondering why this chapter alludes to his awesomeness. When I was seventeen, I had the honor and privilege of working at one of the coolest jobs I have ever had. My still very pseudo punk rock, emo kid self was able to leave TICS and work at a music store. This was my first venture into mall retail. Back then, there were stores other than the big box corporations and Amazon that dedicated themselves to supplying customers solely with the music, movies, and video games that propelled their lives. I'm not being sarcastic when I say that back then music propelled my life. If you remember, I got my first job just to buy a drum set.

> Side note: Some time after I started working at TICS, my parents, namely my mom, realized how important getting a drum set was to me. Knowing this, she pooled all of our external family gift money, and for my birthday, I was gifted with my very own drum set. Yes, I was (and still am) a very lucky kid. But I digress.

We will call my awesome second job Records because even though it no longer exists, I'm sure someone will be offended by my discussion of the actual company. Records is still my favorite job to this day. Not only was I happy to be immersed in the musical culture that I loved, but I was surrounded by like-minded individuals who were as cool as I aspired to be. While working with Alice at TICS, I had made the determination that it was time to leave. I was getting paid minimum wage and hated my job. Sure, I had made an effort to make it easier for both myself and those around me, but that didn't negate the fact that I loathed going to work. Somewhere along the line, someone (I forget who, but probably my mom) reminded me that I could always look for another job. Being new to the working world, it hadn't occurred to me that I didn't have to be stuck working at TICS for the rest of my life.

Armed with the ability to list TICS as my work history, I hit the nearby mall and headed straight to my favorite store. I asked the supervisor at the time if they were hiring, and if I could have an application. I was as dressed up as much as an emo teenager could muster, and I was doing my best to make a good impression. The shift supervisor told me they weren't hiring, but that I could check back next week. She handed me an application and told me I could bring it back whenever. I was heartbroken. Unexperienced and naïve, I assumed getting a job at Records would be as easy as getting my job at TICS. Thankfully, I had not resigned from TICS just yet (but stupidly, I had considered it). Though disappointed, I thanked the shift supervisor for her time, carefully placed the application into a nerdy manila folder, and left the store.

Eager as I was, I filled out the application that night and brought it back the next day. I walked in, again dressed to impress, and asked for the shift supervisor. She wasn't working that day, so I was directed to the store manager. He isn't Chuck Norris, but I'm going to call him Chuck because he is just as awesome and has a very similar likeness in appearance. It's probably the mustache. Anyway, I let Chuck know that the shift supervisor had given me an application the day before, and I had filled it out so that hopefully they would contact me if any positions opened up. Chuck smiled, glanced over my application, and asked me how old I was. I let him know I had just turned seventeen and had a worker's permit (required for anyone in Hawaii to work if they were under eighteen). His face fell a little as he let me know that it was company policy not to hire minors, even with a worker's permit. I was crushed as I had just turned seventeen and would have to wait a whole year to try to get my dream job. Chuck noticed my dismay and let me know he would keep my application on file. Records would be hiring for the holiday season soon, and he thought corporate might overlook my age if I was hired as a seasonal employee. I smiled weakly and thanked him for his time. He encouraged me to come back next week to see if they had any openings yet, and I promised that I would. I went home completely discouraged but being the future-minded teenager that I was, I reminded myself that I could still try and work there in a year. From then on, I made it a goal to constantly remind Chuck that I was enthusiastic about the position.

As I remember it, I would go back to Records on a weekly basis for a while to check in. I don't suggest doing what I did, but I was a high school senior, so going to the mall was a pretty frequent occurrence anyway. I did my best to space out my check-ins, but my anxious teenager heart could only handle about a week between visits. Eventually, the shift supervisors working there came to recognize me and, upon seeing me, let me know nothing was open yet. I didn't even have to ask.

Right before the holiday season was about to hit, I finally got a call back. Chuck seemed happy to finally be able to tell me my constant pestering had paid off. He invited me to come in for an interview and said if I were able to pass the interview, he would work out my age situation with corporate. If I got the job, I would only be a seasonal employee, but he would consider keeping me on after the holidays if I did well. I'm beyond positive that Chuck was trying to get me to stop bugging him, though in conversations I've had with him since he told me my persistence proved I would do everything I could to be a kick-ass employee.

I got through the interview nervously and feeling extremely under qualified, but Chuck gave me a chance, and I was soon officially an underage seasonal employee at Records. I worked my ass off as I was determined to be one of the lucky seasonal employees who got to stick around after January. That determination, coupled with my "working for tips" customer service mentality, seemed to go a long way. I was always on time, happy to stay late, and volunteered for jobs no one wanted to do. I worked as fast as I could to move on to the next project and eventually, I earned my permanent spot on the team.

Working at Records was my dream job because I was surrounded by all things I considered awesome: cool people, good music, and a killer discount. Most importantly, working at Records was made substantially greater because I worked for Chuck. He was good-natured, down-to-earth, professional to customers (but cursed around his employees), and he was a damn good salesman. Chuck was funny and allowed everyone to be weird and "unprofessional" when we weren't dealing with customers. He created an environment that put us at ease, even while we were held to certain sales quotas. I can't imagine that being easy, but he did it.

My favorite memory of Chuck relates to how bad of a salesperson I was. Even though I worked my ass off, when it came to sales, I didn't hit my quotas and would never even imagine exceeding them. Let me explain: I'm sure you've heard of a frequent flyer program, and most companies have some sort of loyalty rewards program they want you to sign up for. The programs usually keep track of how much money you spend with the company and then give you some sort of kick-back for being a loyal customer. Who wouldn't sign up for something like that? Way back when I worked at Records, we had such a program, but unfortunately, it wasn't free. It was about $15 ($14.95 if you buy into that nonsense) and equivalent to the cost of a whole CD or movie. Hard as I tried, I couldn't figure out how to get customers to sign up. I hoped no one would notice I never met my quotas and that they would rationalize that I would make up for it by doing well at everything else. Chuck cared. He cared in the sense that he wanted me to improve not just to keep my job, but because he knew I could do it.

I distinctly remember being terrified of losing my job when Chuck brought me into the back office to discuss my loyalty numbers. I knew I hadn't been performing as well as everyone else, but I also didn't know what I could do about it. Chuck could see I was distraught and let me know immediately that he hadn't brought me to the back office to fire me. All he wanted to do was help. We discussed why I thought I wasn't able to meet my quotas, and this namely boiled down to the fact that I wouldn't buy into the rewards program as a customer based on my own limited funds so I couldn't justify selling it to anyone else. Chuck better understood how I felt, and then proceeded to work with me to overcome my own objections. It was true that someone with limited funding might not want to sign up for a rewards program adding to their expenses, but Chuck pointed out that I was making snap judgments about who might have limited funds just by looking at them. And who was I to make that judgment? We agreed that moving forward, I would ask every customer with the perspective that they could afford the additional cost because, for all I knew, they did. Chuck explained that it was my job to highlight the program in full to every customer. This way, I could inform them about both the cost and benefits of the program to ultimately let them decide for themselves. I wasn't trying to trick anyone into signing up or bullying them into anything they didn't want to do, which is how I had felt previously. I was simply giving them an opportunity to make an informed decision.

I felt so much better after our discussion. Not only was I empowered with new tools to succeed, but I had come to the further realization that Chuck's role was not only disciplinary, but he was also there to support me. Growing up, I was fortunate enough to have both my parents with my mom as the supportive one and my dad as the disciplinarian. I think because of their distributed roles, I thought one person could not provide both support and discipline. With Chuck, I realized not only could one person serve both roles, but that it is absolutely the job of a boss to do so. I miss Chuck a lot, and I now have the undeniable urge to watch Walker Texas Ranger.

So, what did Chuck do right?

This chapter is obviously not about a shitty boss; it's about one of my favorite ones. And there are a lot of things Chuck did well to earn his spot.

Like Chuck Norris, my boss Chuck was a role model. He was someone to look up to not only because he was great at what he did, but because he wanted those around him to succeed as well. He also understood that employees can only be expected to accomplish what they have been trained to do. In the example I discussed, Chuck could have very easily put me on a three strikes type system as a lot of managers are likely to do. After my third "strike" of failing to meet my quota, he would have had grounds to terminate my employment and send me on my way. I'd like to think that I was a good employee and that Chuck recognized the value in retaining me. In reality, I truly believe Chuck would have done the same thing for any other employee because he knew how important it is to invest in your employees. If you want to look at it another way, imagine that you are at a magic show and are suddenly asked to participate as a volunteer. You anxiously take the stage, smiling awkwardly, and hope that nobody needs to get cut in half. The magician then directs you to perform the next trick. He stands next to you waiting while you try figuring out exactly what it is that he wants you to do. There is the added pressure of a restless audience, and you can't even begin to dream up a card trick that might be passable. Working for a boss that just expects you to know how to do something without giving you any direction is kind of like this magician we're talking about. To be fair, most magicians won't put audience members on the spot like that. They'll tell them exactly what they want them to do giving them step by step directions because they know they are also tasked with keeping the audience entertained. As a non-magical volunteer, you'd likely focus intently (so as not to embarrass yourself) and do exactly as you are told. Then, you pull a rabbit out of a hat, and the volunteer and the magician have completed the magic trick. Presto! There's obviously a lot more to a magic trick than that, but I'm no magician.

Chuck was a managerial magician, and he better understood that practice always helped. Using the same scenario, if you, the volunteer, were to practice the trick over and over and over again, eventually you would get to the point where you didn't need the magician. Chuck understood he had to put in some time and practice to truly support his employees, and he did this whenever someone needed it. He was extremely busy as the store manager, so when he couldn't get to something, he made sure that his second in command (the shift supervisor) was ready to step in and support in the same way. He trusted her immensely, and she thrived when he empowered her.

Earlier I explained that a good boss is someone who can be supportive, but also provide discipline. While Chuck was great at helping to train and coach us, he was also very vocal and strict about things he would not tolerate. He was transparent about the behaviors that were unacceptable during the workday, such as being disrespectful to customers or other employees or being excessively late. It didn't matter how long you had worked at Records or how well you did at selling the loyalty program. If you did not follow one of the rules, you were going to have a discussion about it. I was smart enough to always follow the rules so I couldn't tell you what happened personally, but I always remembered Chuck did not play favorites. He (and everyone else) considered his rules to be pretty simple and understandable, and he didn't care if you were the shift supervisor or a seasonal employee; the rules applied to everyone. I appreciated that he didn't attempt to sweep bad behaviors "under the rug" for higher ranked employees, but that he addressed them straight on and took care of them before they turned into bigger problems.

Another great thing about Chuck was his sense of humor and his decision to let comedy drive his managerial style. Chuck could talk a lot of shit and was more than able to take it right back. While Chuck wouldn't ever curse in front of a customer, he swore (for emphasis and comedic relief) in front of the team regularly. This somehow gave us a more realistic perspective of Chuck. He was a flawed human like the rest of us who liked to jest with other employees and didn't mind if another employee poked fun of him. I believe that because our team was able to laugh together, we began to feel a sense of community and worked well together because of it. Just a note because you don't know Chuck, but he would never swear at us when working with us on an area of improvement. We weren't called idiots or morons because we didn't know how to do something. He knew where the line was and stayed clearly on the correct side of it.

One of my favorite parts of working at Records (aside from the amazing discount) was that we all went by weird, random nicknames - nicknames that have lasted for over fifteen years. To this day, I am still in touch with a good amount of my Records coworkers, and they still refer to me by my nickname. Our nicknames were so pervasive that if I were to introduce someone new to my former Records coworkers, I would likely blank on their real names. It is still so weird to me that the guy I know as Noodle (seriously, that's his real nickname) is now a legislative attorney. While you may think that nicknames are a little silly, I believe they helped to instill camaraderie and quickly build rapport. It's difficult to think someone is threatening if their nickname is "Eesh" or "Lala". Learning our nicknames was a quick way into our Records community, which we all cherished and respect to this day.

Did it work?

Perhaps you are wondering if all of these weird, awesome techniques Chuck used actually did us any good? The answer is an emphatic yes! Our Records location was the top-selling location in our district. Our district became the top seller in the region, and ultimately, the top seller in the nation. We were pretty badass, probably because Chuck Norris was our boss. There are a lot of variables that go into determining a "top selling" store but knowing that we were ranked the best of the best was and is a good indication to me that our Records store had something special.

Honestly, if you have a boss like Chuck, do your best to never leave your job and learn everything that you can from them. I was fortunate enough to work with Chuck both at Records and then later at a big box store that he was kind enough to suggest I apply for. We had some great times as a team, and I value the lessons I learned as an employee as well as those I learned when eventually tasked to lead others. Thanks for everything, Chuck - I probably wouldn't be writing this if not for you.

What Would Chuck Do? (WWCD)

Instead of asking questions about how you might be a Shitty Boss or an Asshole Employee, this time around, I'm going to give you a brief scenario and ask you "What Would Chuck Do?" It is then your job to put yourself in Chuck's perspective to figure out how you think he might have handled the scenario. Ready?

Scenario 1: Loss Prevention

Pretend you are Chuck. You have just witnessed one of your employees act in the name of "Loss Prevention" by verbally accusing a customer of stealing from the store. The company policy indicates that you cannot address an individual's intention to steal - you must wait until they physically steal the product by carrying it out of the store, at which point mall security can detain them. Your employee has technically not followed the policy but also has prevented a theft from occurring. If you were Chuck, how would you react?

1. Based on the way you think Chuck would respond to the scenario, consider how you would have responded and compare Chuck's response to yours. Are they similar? Why or why not?
2. Based on your comparison, are there any new ideas that you can implement in your current position? What issue(s) are you trying to solve for?

Scenario 2: Black Friday

Imagine it's the day after Thanksgiving and Black Friday is upon you. It is the biggest retail day of the year when everyone officially kicks off their Christmas shopping. You have carefully and proactively planned out your staff, so everyone knows what their tasks will be once customers hit your store. As you arrive at the store bright and early at 4:00 a.m., you begin to receive text messages in quick succession from not one but three of the five staff members you had scheduled to help you to open the store. They all spent Thanksgiving together, and all are now dealing with food poisoning. You go into a quick panic and then take a breath. What the hell are you going to do?

It's a retail nightmare. You are figuratively preparing for a customer service war, and you are outnumbered and outmanned. You go into high gear and survey the two employees who are half awake. You quickly, but calmly explain to them what has happened. Knowing that you can't keep the store closed on the busiest day of the year, what do you do next?

1. Of the two employees, one is seasonal, meaning that they have never worked a Black Friday in your store. The other is experienced and one of your best employees. Knowing what you know, would you ask your employees for their opinions, or would you dictate a game plan to them? What would Chuck have done? How do they compare?

You decide that you will manage the already growing line of customers outside of your door. You bring them coupons and let them all know in advance that due to Thanksgiving food poisoning you are severely understaffed. You also hand out pieces of paper and pencils, asking the customers who are in line to write down the items (in priority) that they know they are there to purchase. You walk down the line of 50 people and then race back to the front to gather orders. You ask each customer to write down their name on their order and to have a form of ID ready when they enter the store. They are welcome to peruse the store or go straight to the register to purchase their items. Since you already staged the store and are ready to open at 6:00 a.m., you task your two employees with gathering the product for each order, and ring them up in suspended mode (tallying all current items but allowing the order to be changed once a customer intends to pay). In essence, once customers enter the store, half of the work is already done. Your employees look relieved as they get to work, and you breathe a little easier as you go back out to collect additional orders. You've effectively figured out what to do, and once the store opens, the day goes smoothly until shifts are about to change. Your customers are appreciative of your ingenuity, and you highly consider going this route again next year.

2. Based on the day you've had, you more than deserve to head straight home and take a nice long nap but haven't described your plans to your shift supervisor who is set to replace you at the shift change. Do you go home? If not, what do you do? What would Chuck do?

Final Thoughts

I promise on all that is Disney that both of these scenarios are entirely made up, but they are also completely feasible. For those of you that haven't worked in retail, it may be a little more difficult to understand the ferocity that can sometimes occur, but you can likely understand the amount of quick decision making that needs to happen. Operating from this time crunch perspective can sometimes motivate you and your team to work together and bring you closer together, as a result. It can be an extremely stressful situation, but a good manager knows how to support their employees in a way that makes them feel empowered while meeting the overall team goals.

The next chapter is about what happens when you go from an awesome boss you love to a shitty boss that you hate, and how your frustrations are imposed on the new boss, sometimes for things that they cannot help.

CHAPTER 3:
When the Music Dies, and Scarface is Not Just a Movie

I've been told that all good things must come to an end, and I have never believed a statement to be more true (except maybe the ones about gravity and global warming). When it comes to bosses, Chuck was one of the best, so it was a very sad day when I found out that he was leaving us. I would have been happy for him if he had found something that deserved his many talents and people management skills, but unfortunately Records Corporate had determined that he was no longer fit to serve as our store manager. The specifics of the situation are entirely ridiculous from my perspective, and they shouldn't have let him go. It was unfair, and I resented Records Corporate for making such an asinine move. Fortunately, our shift supervisor, who was now the Assistant Store Manager was still around, and she kept the store together while Records Corporate searched for a replacement Store Manager. I wish they would have just let her take the position, but then we wouldn't have the following story to discuss.

Eventually, Records Corporate found Chuck's replacement, and she wreaked of lies from the moment she set foot in the store. I want to tell you that I was mature and tried to give her the benefit of the doubt, but by then I was still only eighteen and hated Records Corporate for taking Chuck away, only to replace him with this lying puppet. We called her Scarface, because honestly, we were a bunch of immature asshole employees. For the sake of dignity however, I'm going to call her Janice.

By the time Janice started working for Records, the Assistant Store Manager had done a good job of keeping the store running, and we were still number one across the board in our district and region. Most of us were still pretty sullen about Chuck, but we liked our jobs for the most part and hadn't made any moves to leave. Janice quickly changed our minds about staying.

Aside from the overall annoyance that Janice presented, there are a couple of stories in particular that I remember from working with her. If you haven't seen the movie Empire Records, do yourself a favor and go watch it. I'll warn you in advance that it's pretty teen-angsty and not really at all what it's like to work in a music store, but it resonated with me when I, as a self-proclaimed emo kid, worked at Records the summer after high school ended. I remember thinking that our little store was kind of like what the movie strived to be and enjoyed that I could plug myself into this little piece of pop culture. Knowing all of this, keep in mind that I never imagined, or even gave anyone the impression that I was somehow connected to the movie, other than as a patron. The most ridiculous lie that Janice ever told me was that the movie was based on her and her friends back from when she used to work at a different music store. She brazenly explained to me how the writers of the movie had tried to capture her in one character, but that ultimately her personality could be found in all of the characters. We do drug testing for retail jobs. This lady was not high when she told me this, she was just a straight up liar. I couldn't believe that an adult (back then she had to have been at least 35) was making such an outlandish claim right to my face. The very polite and Asian part of my brain imagined flipping her off and laughing directly in her face. The outward professional raised an accusative eyebrow and walked away to find someone to gossip with. Was she serious? Did she just claim to have been the inspiration for all of the characters in Empire Records? For a moment, I wondered if she was mentally unstable, and then promptly realized that I really just didn't care. In my book, telling a lie like that speaks volumes about your character. (I understand the irony of that sentence only now.) You are either in dire need of some medication to be prescribed only by a licensed psychiatrist, or you are so brutally self-conscious and insecure about not being accepted or liked, that you make up implausible stories in hopes that someone will believe you for long enough to be your friend. Janice was, without a drop of doubt, the latter.

There is a reason that confidence is valued by the American culture, if only because the opposite insecurities manifest themselves in the most clingy, sticky, and deplorable manners. And this is coming from someone who has self-diagnosed anxiety and is forever self-conscious about the things I say and do. I know when my self-consciousness is unrelenting. I can feel the self-hate bubbling up, but I can't stop it. Still, I have never come to a point where I have felt the need to spew such undeniable bull shit. A lie like that just screams to others that you want so badly to be accepted that you will say and do anything in your power to earn that acceptance. The truly unfortunate thing is that the revolting smell of this desire for acceptance is what drives everyone else away and contributes to the unending vicious cycle. Janice couldn't help but try to impress us, but all it did was cause our team to have less and less...and then, even less respect for her. Janice, I do pity you. I understand where the self-loathing comes from on a personal level. But seriously, the lies didn't do you any favors.

You know how you walk into a room, and it suddenly becomes quiet, and you wonder if the sudden drop in volume is because the occupants of the room, yourself excluded, were previously discussing you in a manner so disrespectful that even they knew they needed to shut the hell up? Most of the time the silence is likely an evolved response, and people aren't actually talking shit about you. At least that is what I tell myself. In Janice's case, she was almost always interrupting some level of vile shit talking. On the one hand, yes, we were despicable people who probably should have been a little more understanding of this poor woman who definitely couldn't help herself. On the other, we were a couple of college-aged kids who had just lost the best boss we had ever known and were given a less than worthy replacement. Most of the time I helped to close the store, and after all of our customers had left and we'd cleaned up and replaced product, we usually locked up and hung out upstairs in the rooftop parking lot and decompressed from our day. We had done this when Chuck was around, and usually just bitched and moaned about some annoying customer. Once Janice started, she was almost always the focal point of our discussion. Deserved or not, we couldn't stand her.

Back when I used to work at Records, new media would be released on Tuesdays. This meant that on Monday night after the store was closed, we would put out the newly released music, movies, and video games on display in the storefront window. Sometimes new C.D.'s would come with cardboard displays that needed to be built, and advertisement signage always needed to be replaced. After working at Records for a while, I was often tasked with handling the new releases, and I had a system down. I would be scheduled to close the store on Monday nights, and I would spend the latter part of the shift preparing all of the merchandise to be put out while emptying the storefront shelving. I prepped "Sale" stickers, took down signage, and readied any cardboard displays. Once we closed, I would quickly replace signs, and load the product into the window. I had a routine going that the other managers appreciated and trusted. I was pretty proud of the responsibility, and further liked the added perk of seeing new release product a little ahead of some of the other employees.

When Janice started, one of the first things that she decided that she was going to change was the way that we handled new release Tuesdays. Shocker, right? I obviously wouldn't have explained all of that if it wasn't about to get royally screwed up. Anyway...Janice decided that she would take over handling new releases, and not only did she take the responsibility away from me, but she also took me off of the Monday night shift. She essentially said that I was an extra body that didn't need to work that night if I wasn't going to be preparing for new release Tuesday. It didn't matter that I could have just worked the shift as normal.

I walked in on Tuesday morning (remember that it was summer, so I didn't have any school) ready to judge how Janice had handled new releases. I was expecting an incorrect sign, or some of the merchandise from the previous week's release to still be on display. Minor accidents that most customers wouldn't have noticed. Janice did not disappoint: none of the signs had been replaced, none of the new merchandise was on shelf, none of the old merchandise had been taken down, and the cardboard display for that week's Brittney Spears new C.D. release (probably, I'm guessing on this one) was still unassembled in a box in the back office. Janice hadn't prepped for the new release the night before. She had expected to come into the store as scheduled on Tuesday morning, prepare the registers to be used for the day, and set up the new releases before the store opened. To be fair, this is not undoable, and if she had help from other employees, her plan could have worked. What Janice did not account for, was the fact that she had never done a new release Tuesday ad set before. An ad set is a set of instructions, sent from Records Corporate, that literally has a picture which details how a window display should look. They do this so that all locations can look uniform and customers have the same "great" experience whether they are visiting a store in Hawaii or California. If you've never read an ad set before, it can be a little confusing, and Janice had lied on her resume. She had apparently never done an ad set before, even though she had supposedly managed the would-be Empire Records. And of course, smart as Janice thought she was, she had supposed that because some high school kid could do the ad set with no problems, that she would have no issue either.

Part of me wanted to scoff in her face, and then point and laugh at her uncontrollably. What a moron! The other, very Type-A part of me that takes extreme pride in my work...well that part of me was angry and wanted to scream. Even though I guarantee none of our customers knew that I was the employee that set up new releases and that there was no way that I would get any blame for what was happening, I was embarrassed and frustrated. I had worked hard to consistently do a good job at merchandising for the ad set, and in one fell swoop, Janice had ruined my clean record. Not only that, but customers were starting to complain. They were wondering where the newest albums were, and our regular customers were wondering why the window display hadn't been reset. Janice looked around bewildered as she continued to attempt to ready the ad, even though the store had already been open for about an hour.

Did I forget to mention this? Yes, I think so. The evil, immature asshole that I am, I had gone into Records ON MY DAY OFF just to see the shit show. I had literally crawled out of bed before noon in the middle of summer just to see how craptacular my new boss was. You can feel free to judge me and realize what a jerk I am.

Hopefully, I will redeem myself by telling you that even though I was not scheduled to work that day, when Janice caught sight of me, she rushed over and in pure panic mode, she asked me to help her with the ad set. Before I could say anything, she let me know that she would make sure I got paid for however long I was there to help. And yes, this evil, immature asshole decided to help. I didn't even try to drag out my time to get paid a little more. I just helped out because it was the right thing to do, and I honestly had a lot of pride in my job. I know, weird right? Like I said, hopefully I've redeemed myself.

After I had helped Janice out with the ad set, she somehow thought that it meant that we were friends. Remember that I had walked into the store to find evidence of her terrible job and that I had really only helped begrudgingly so that the store wouldn't look bad. No part of me was trying to be friends with the store enemy, but Janice persisted. I soon realized that she was also trying to befriend the rest of the team. They were equally as unamused as I was. She attempted to make up inside-jokes that didn't catch on. She tried to give herself a nickname, like the rest of the team, even though she unknowingly already had one. She tried to hang out on the rooftop parking lot when we closed the store. All of this was to no avail. We didn't trust her or respect her, and we quite frankly just didn't like being around her. Her self-doubt made us all extremely uncomfortable, and nobody wants to voluntarily put up with that.

Eventually, her antics got to the point where we all became extremely frustrated with her, and slowly the team started to find jobs elsewhere until the majority of us no longer worked at Records anymore. It was kind of like the end of Sandlots where the narrator is telling you where each character ends up, as they slowly fade out of the scene. Without the team there to drive our loyalty sales, our Records location began to drop in the district and the region. And I'm not saying that our team was holding that company together, because let's be honest, it was the economic culture shift in the way that consumers obtain their music, but Records, as a company no longer exists. They were bought out by another now failing company, just a couple of months after the last of our team left. I'm telling you, Records Corporate should have never let go of Chuck. Chuck Norris was keeping music (sales) alive! Kidding, obviously. Music is not and will never actually be dead.

So, what did Janice do wrong?

If you answered A LOT, then you are absolutely correct! Based on the handful of stories I've shared with you, I'm sure you can guess a few things. To start, one of the worst things you can do is lie. And not only that but tell a lie that is so blatantly false that no one is going to even try and believe you. Why seriously WHY would you lie about being the inspiration for a movie? Even if it might be true, it's so hard to believe that you should at least attempt to establish some foundation of trust before you drop that weirdo bomb on a person. That's one of those stories that you tell after you've known a person for a while and they trust you when it comes to simple facts like your occupation, or age, or you've showcased your dependability in some way. If you tell someone something like that, you should give them no cause for pause when they ask themselves why you would be lying about it. For example, we've been through a couple of chapters by now, and I think I've built up some trust with you as a reader. If I were to tell you that I play five instruments, you would probably have an easy time believing me, right? If I told you that during my introduction chapter, for no real reason, you would probably think I was a crazy person and wonder why I offered up that information totally unsolicited. The point is: don't lie. Don't tell lies that don't make any sense. When you lie to people that are supposed to rely on you and trust you; you are setting that professional relationship up for failure. Either the lie is so unbelievable that they will no longer believe anything else you tell them, or the lie is believable at first, but the truth will eventually come out, and then your people will feel betrayed and lose any respect they had for you. Just don't do it. It doesn't do you any good.

Janice, if you remember, also had a terrible case of self-doubt. She didn't respect herself and was in such dire need for attention and friendship that she was almost whiny about her desire to be accepted. Now, I'm going to take a breath before I offer up the next piece of advice, just honestly because I am terrible at following it: Just be yourself. I know that everybody says this, but I guess, more than being yourself (because who else could you be), what you need to do is accept yourself. I don't mean that you need to think that you are awesome and the best thing since the invention of the wheel. What I mean to say is that you need to be honest with yourself about your strengths and applaud yourself for them, while also being aware of and honest about your weaknesses, and then be forgiving and kind to yourself. For example, I am terrible at exercising. I absolutely hate it! Does that mean the rest of who I am sucks? I guess it depends on who you ask, haha. Seriously though, hating exercise doesn't make me a bad person. It just means that it's something that I can stand to work on. And I should work to accept that. That's a little off topic, but the point is that you need to own up to your faults and be honest about them. If you can have that level of self-awareness, it is likely that your team will recognize your self-security. And you will be that much closer to earning their trust.

From a non-be-your-best-you perspective, another practical thing that Janice could have done is trusted the system that was in place. We talked about this when we discussed Alice in the first chapter, but I'll repeat myself because I can't stress it enough. If you are new to a position or a company in general, you do not need to rush into your job, full steam ahead with amazing new ideas. You do not have to make changes immediately. Maybe you think that you've been told by your own new boss that the reason you've been hired is to "clean house" and fix the many problems that exist. You might want to consider that your new boss may not have been working directly with the folks that you are now going to be responsible for managing. They also may have heard terrible things about these people from the person who was in your position previously. Or they could be a terrible boss themselves, and eager to place blame on subordinates instead of taking ownership of their piece of the problem. The truth is that there are many variables that factor into a problem, and when you are removed from it, it can be easy to place blame on the people involved. And this happens even if blame would be more rightfully placed on the procedure, resources, or equipment that those people must work with.

I'm sure that someone at the corporate level had told Janice that the ad set shift that I worked was an extraneous cost that needed to be incorporated into the regular shifts. Someone probably even told her that the ad set could easily be done on Tuesday morning by a competent manager, instead of having a shift (a whole 8 hours of minimum wage) dedicated to merchandising. I understand that it can be difficult to hear something like that and not immediately try to make a "simple" change that will help to quickly impress your new superiors. But what I am telling you is that change is never simple. There will always be some kind of effect from the change that you implement, good or bad, and that it is in your best interest to do your homework ahead of time. In the example I explained, Janice ended up paying for the additional help anyway. Sure, the amount of time was decreased in comparison to the full 8-hour shift, and likely prettied up the bottom line, but making the thoughtless change cost her the respect that she could have earned.

So, what should Janice have done differently?
There are some simple suggestions that I would have given to Janice had I been a nicer and more mature person at the time. Truthfully, at Records, we were the Mean Girls and we had effectively told Janice that she couldn't sit with us. Of course, there are things that she could have done that would have made it a lot easier for us to be nicer to her, and I'll go into those in a bit, but in reflecting back on my time working with Janice, I realize now that I was pretty much a total asshole. I couldn't stand her for so many personality-related reasons that she probably couldn't have helped. I mean, it's not like you can just suddenly

change your personality to fit your new job. And Janice was not a mean person. She was just terrible at integrating into our team.

Records Corporate could have done a better job of replacing Chuck, but they were so removed from us that there was no way for them to know what kind of store manager our team needed. They needed to understand the type of culture that exists in a music store, and more importantly, the type of people. If you can detail the profile of your employees, you will likely do a better job of supporting them. When I worked at Records, I honestly thought I had finally achieved the level of "cool" that I had been working to attain all throughout high school. I had older friends, I cursed like a sailor, and I wore black all the time. (Yes, my definition of "cool" was a little bit skewed.) In my own under-aged, still developing mind, I was a rebel and was looking for an opportunity to "stick it to the man." Feel free to laugh at this, I know that I do. The truth is that I was only as "cool" as I had ever been, which wasn't very, but I had found the place where I belonged. And armed with my weird nickname and "fuck the corporations" attitude, I was primed to be pissed off at Janice from the start. I'm going to generalize here, and you can feel free to judge, but I don't really think that my misfit perspective was all that different from many of the other kids my age. I think that most "almost adults" take on this attitude at some point in time. I'm getting a little off topic, but the point is that Records Corporate could have come to the realization that they were likely employing a ton of emo kids, and that maybe it might have been a good idea to find someone who wouldn't give them another reason to be pissed off at the world.

A classmate from my doctoral program once told me that during an interview, she was asked if she knew what a flux capacitor was. I thought it was ingenious. Such a simple question easily weeded out potential candidates based on the idea of culture fit. If a candidate didn't know what a flux capacitor was, they would have had a harder time integrating into the existing team. All my bitching about Records Corporate is basically to say that they should have added a culture-related question to their selection process (along with a lie detector test) and maybe they would have hired someone more suited to manage us.

I know that I've been complaining about Records Corporate, and not about Janice, but I'll get to that. I just wanted to make the point that sometimes it is not a candidate's fault that they are not a good fit for a company, but rather it is a faulty selection process that allows them to be hired that may be to blame. Anyway, moving on...

While Records Corporate could have done better, Janice brought her own additional problems to the table. The lying is an obvious thing to fix. I know that you maybe shouldn't share every last bit of information with your subordinates, but that does not mean that you should make up outlandish stories. If you're considering it, first ask yourself what you really have to gain in the long term by telling your weird ass story. Because if you're lying to get attention, you don't deserve it. Additionally, I know that the self-conscious need to be liked is something that most of us can't do anything about. Hell, if you have a cure for that, please send it my way. But what we can do, and what I have done personally, is be as upfront and honest about the things that you think people shouldn't like about you. Most of the time, you will find that people will accept you for your flaws, and maybe even like you for them. I know, people are weird. What people don't like is when you put on a show and layer yourself with bullshit and ridiculousness. Could Janice have stopped being anxious and clingy? Probably not, and that's a rough situation to be in. But could she have recognized these things about herself, and let people know in advance that she has those tendencies? Absolutely. I have a tendency to talk too much and swear all the time, two things that I know can annoy and offend people. So what do I do about it? I know that I won't even realize I'm doing it, so I tell people that I have these tendencies, but that I don't mean to offend them. I also give them free reign to tell me when I am talking too much or being offensive. That way, they can deal with a situation that makes them uncomfortable. If Janice had told all of us up front that she was nervous about starting and that she really wanted our help to do a good job, it would have gone a long way towards a more positive working environment.

One last thing that Janice could have done differently is something that Alice also could have improved on. I'll even break it down into three general steps:

1. Observe: Upon entering a new position or organization, take the time to learn about your new environment. Talk to the people that already work there and get a good understanding of what happens on a day to day, week to week, month to month basis and so on. Learning about the history of your team can help you to understand where they came from, what they might have overcome, and hopefully what they are capable of. There is a reason that we study history in school so that we don't repeat the same mistakes over and over again. Taking the time to understand your team also gives you the opportunity to build much-needed rapport. They will appreciate that you are trying to understand them and begin to trust you.

2. Evaluate: Once you have an idea of what the team is like, and their history, you can then start to work with them to figure out what is or isn't working efficiently. Listen to their perspective and ideas, because they are the people who are actually doing the processes that you are talking about improving. And they will know better than anyone else how to fix it. There will be processes that they may not think needs improvement because they have been very close to these processes and may not realize that there are

more efficient ways to do things. But don't assume automatically that you know better than they do.

3. Implement: After you have taken the previously described steps, that's when it makes sense to implement new changes. At this point, you've taken the time to understand your team, understand their perspectives and concerns. You've asked them for their advice on what can be better. With all of this initial input, you've built rapport, and you've established buy-in. They are more likely to be supportive of the changes by this time because truly, they have helped you to decide what those changes should be.

I'm not saying that these steps are easy, and they are difficult to do if you have already been a shitty boss, but if Janice had one day decided to start asking what I thought about how to make improvements at Records, I would have been intrigued. I wouldn't have trusted her at first, and anything I would have offered up would have been small because I wouldn't want to get my hopes up. But if she had then followed through and implemented a positive change based on my suggestion, the next time she would have asked, I would have been that much more likely to offer something up. Doing these steps can slowly help to rebuild trust, as long as you are sure to follow through with implementations together. It's by no means an easy path to take, but it makes all the difference between leading based purely on a status that was given to you or leading based on the trust and respect that your team has for you.

So...what?: Survival Skills

Hopefully, we can agree that Janice wasn't the worst person in the world (even though I definitely thought so back then). She just wasn't the right person for the job for a number of reasons. It doesn't really matter though, because as a subordinate, you don't have a lot of control over your boss. The only person you really have any control over is yourself, and even though that may sound relatively simple, it's actually a huge pain in the ass.

In retrospect, there were a couple of things that I could have done that might have made my life a lot easier and would have helped Janice out. For starters, I needed to change my attitude. I could have decided that even though Chuck was no longer around, that didn't have to mean that Janice was going to be a terrible replacement. I still believe that she was, but I didn't have to believe that right from the get-go. I could have given her a chance, difficult as it would have been. Like we discussed with Alice, in the same way that a new boss should take some time to get a feel for their new environment, an employee who is dealing with that new boss should give them the time to acclimate. When you are first learning how to do your job, you are bound to make mistakes. You wouldn't be human if you didn't. A boss is human and therefore, will make mistakes. As an employee, once you've checked your attitude, you can then have some sympathy for your new boss and even more importantly, be forgiving.

I'm not saying to forgive everything. I'm saying that you can't hold every last thing that they do wrong against them. All you would be doing at that point is harboring a level of hate that is unhealthy from a physical and mental perspective. If your boss just can't seem to figure out the ad set, maybe that is frustrating and a little unforgivable because it's a competency she should have been hired with. On the other hand, if she doesn't know how to stop talking when you are working the same shift as her, that's probably something that you should forgive. It's irritating, but something that she shouldn't be judged harshly for when it comes to her job duties. If you want your boss to respect you, then you owe them a certain level of respect in return.

Going along the lines of giving your boss a chance, another thing that you can do is to pay close attention to the new changes and ideas that your boss is suggesting. Granted, they might all be total crap because your boss has no idea what they are doing, but if you are trying to find a good idea, instead of immediately looking for a bad idea, you will have an easier time reconciling your frustration. If you can't find a "good idea," then you can also identify the good parts of an idea. There are bound to be some. Once you've located a good idea or part of one, you can give out a compliment and discuss the good idea. You can also then use that compliment as a pivotal point of the conversation to give some suggestions of your own. This can help to soften the blow a little bit. Bosses that think a little too highly of themselves often get defensive when you offer up suggestions or criticisms, and rather than hearing what you have to say, they will shut down and ignore you. This can be extremely frustrating when you feel like you are just trying to help. If you were to approach your boss with suggestions that improve on their idea in the guise of a compliment, they may be a little more willing to let you take the lead on the changes.

To tell you the absolute truth, these suggestions are just based on how I would appreciate being told that my ideas are crap. Help me to realize why, and then help me so that we can make the changes together. The contrasting perspective, where you aggressively point out that your boss is incompetent, while it might be more cathartic for you as an employee, it will not serve a positive result in the long term. As an employee, you've lost the trust of your boss and likely the respect along with it. Rebuilding that trust takes a lot of time when you could have just listened first.

Now, I'm not a total idiot, and I absolutely understand that my suggestions for "managing up" sound a lot like brown nosing or kissing ass. And to a certain extent, you wouldn't be wrong about that. When everyone else is frustrated with a new boss, and you decide to either remain neutral or even (gasp) be helpful, you can look and feel like you are trying to be the teacher's pet. If that makes you uncomfortable, I totally understand. You want to continue to be a part of the in-group with the rest of your coworkers, instead of crossing the picket lines. Maybe it's because of self-preservation, or maybe you really can't see beyond your frustrations – which is not a judgment because I have totally been there. But the reality is that when both sides of the table cross their arms over their chests and put their noses in the air, nobody is getting anywhere. It takes a person who can see both sides, who can extend the olive branch, to work towards something that is productive.

That might not be you. Honestly, most of the time, I am not that person. I am the first one to respond with anger and frustration. But I'm trying to learn that responding that way isn't helpful. Does it make me feel a hell of a lot better? Sure, maybe for the moment. But all I've done is put the other party on defense mode, which makes it that much more difficult to collaborate. Remaining calm and looking for the areas where ideas and intentions overlap can be helpful. You can go home and vent your frustrations out to your significant other, your dog, or even a dartboard that would have a picture of your boss's face on it. I'm just kidding, I promise I don't have a dartboard...or a dog for that matter. What I mean to say, is that there is a time and place for yelling, screaming and generally acting like a child. You deserve to, so go ahead, just don't do it at work. Voice your concerns in a way that is as helpful as possible to the team AND to the overall situation. Again, I am not usually this person, but I am trying to be. And for your sake, you should consider it.

Ask yourself...do you feel lucky?

Now comes the part of the chapter where you really should ask yourself how you play a role in your own frustration, whether you are the Shitty Boss or the Asshole Employee. Maybe you are both? It's totally possible.

Shitty Boss:
1) We talked about how Janice has some personality defects that absolutely annoyed my coworkers and I, namely being needy for acceptance. You probably have some aspect of your personality that may rub people the wrong way. It doesn't have to be something that is actually bad. For example, you could be an extremely happy and optimistic person, but it annoys people who are self-proclaimed realists. The point here is to be self-aware of the effect that you have on others.
   a. So, what part of your personality has annoyed someone in the past? Like I said, it doesn't have to be a bad thing. But is it? Do you consider this to be something that might even bug you about yourself?
   b. If it is something you want to improve on, how are you working on that? What else could you do?
   c. If it is something that isn't something you want to change, but you know it can rub people the wrong way, why do you think it annoys them? Understanding why may help you to better relate to them.
2) Let's talk about lying because everybody does it. What kind of lies do you tell? Lies to get attention? To protect others (a.k.a. white lies)? To make yourself look good? Omitted lies because topics are sensitive? Over generalizations that don't actually tell anybody the truth? (Yes, I consider that to be deceptive, and very much like a lie.) You probably tell some different kinds of lies, so figure out why you tell them.
   a. If you lie to get attention or to make yourself look good, why do you do that? Are you self-conscious about something? If so, what?

b. If you lie to protect others, is the lie actually protecting them? Or are you trying to avoid a conflict?

c. If you are over-generalizing, is it because you don't want to deal with the fallout from the truth?

3) And the last question, by this point, do you understand why it's important to gather information before making a change (small or large)? If not, please refer back to "So, what should Janice have done differently?" and read up on the Observe, Evaluate, and Implement Steps until they are drilled into your head. You may not always have the time, but at least making an attempt to do these steps can be helpful.

Asshole Employee:

1) If your boss annoys you, have you pinpointed exactly why? Is it based on their general personality? Or is it because you feel like they don't respect you?

a. If it's because of their personality, what is it about their personality that sucks? Once you've figured that out, ask yourself if it's truly unforgivable, or just a clash against your personality? Are you a pessimist vs. an optimist? Are you an introvert vs. an extrovert? Is this something that should continue to frustrate you, or something that you should learn to accept because people are allowed to be different from each other?

b. If it's because you feel disrespected, what has your boss done to disrespect you? Do they ignore your suggestions? Do they disregard past accomplishments? Have they overhauled something that you used to manage? I'm not saying that any of these things are fair, but how much of your frustration is based on your ego, and how much of it is your boss just not knowing any better?

2) Now, understanding how your boss might be pissing you off, what can you do to reconcile your frustration? Like we discussed, you don't have any control over what your boss does, but you can control how you react to the situation. So, what can you do to calm yourself down? How can you make attempts to look at the situation overall?
3) Going back to a boss that is making changes too quickly, can you understand what might be driving that change? Is it because they are being pressured by their boss? Is it because they are trying to make improvements? Most of the time, bosses are not making frivolous changes to make themselves look good (even though that's how it may feel), so can you figure out what their motivation might be?
   a. Once you recognize their motivation, can you understand it?

I had tried to spread out the bad bosses and the good bosses, but unfortunately, I have not had that many great bosses in the retail part of my working life, so the next chapter is about another shitty boss. If you're still here, thanks for sticking with me. I promise the next chapter will be "short."

CHAPTER 4:
Retail Napoleon

For reasons that you will soon find out, we will call my next boss Napoleon. I was about 19 when I found a new job, working as a cashier at another, larger retail location. I was incredibly sad to leave Records, where I had established great relationships with my coworkers and had a killer discount. But my new job paid me a whopping $1.50 more per hour, and I was excited to be paid more than minimum wage. Leaving Janice behind was also a pretty huge plus. My new position was with a big box office supply retailer that we will call Paper Cuts, and a friend from high school had helped me to get the job, by telling me how to "cheat" on the application survey. At the time, I had thought it was a bit scandalous, but now, years later, I'm sure it was actually harmless. I'll let you in on the secret because it was kind of a silly gatekeeper. When you take a survey that asks you if you Strongly Disagree, Disagree, Are Neutral, Agree, or Strongly Agree, a lot of time applicants will tend to stay in the middle three options (Disagree, Neutral, or Agree). Most humans understand that there is a certain amount of gray in every situation, so they don't necessarily want to commit to saying that they Strongly Disagree or Strongly Agree. The trick is that if you want to work at Paper Cuts, you have to choose one of those 'Strong' options. You have to indicate that you Strongly Agree that showing up to work late is unacceptable, even though you know that there are times when showing up to work late might be due to an emergency or something unforeseeable. Simply limiting your answers to one of these two options, and having some common sense, would likely have helped you to also get an interview at Paper Cuts. Luckily, I was told this in advance, and after an uneventful interview I started working as a cashier.

Working at Paper Cuts was different from working at Records in the sense that at Records, there was always something to do, and more importantly, always something that needed to be completed by a certain time. Everyone chipped in to help because there were usually only two or three of us working a shift. At Paper Cuts, we had multiple departments and required at least one employee to work in each department. We had cashiers, technology sales, furniture sales, stockers, a couple of managers, sometimes a person to run the warehouse in the back, and my favorite department, Copy and Print. Everyone was usually limited to understanding their roles and responsibilities as it related to their specific department. Cashiers wouldn't help to restock product because that is what the stockers did. Technology Sales employees didn't run a register, because they had to make sure to push their technology sales. Every once and a while a manager would have a good understanding of how to help out in all of the departments, but more often than not, managers also stuck to their areas of expertise.

Having worked at Records, where we were all cross-trained on how to do multiple jobs throughout the store, I would end up being really bored at Paper Cuts. Running a register isn't rocket science if you know how to count change, and are accustomed to offering additional frequent shopper programs, both of which I already knew how to do. And I was efficient about it. Working at Paper Cuts taught me how to manage a line, which is essentially a large group of people who are sometimes frustrated while they wait in a somewhat orderly fashion to accomplish something. If you can see all of them, and regularly let them know that you appreciate them for waiting, they tend to be less angry when they get to you. Customers also tend to be way less pissed off if they don't think you are taking your time with every customer in line before you get to them. They can usually recognize efficiency, and they appreciate it. They also feel sympathy for you when you are the only person running a register (as fast as you can), or if they can see that the only other cashier is taking their sweet ass time. Sometimes humans can suck, and other times they can be so undeservedly forgiving.

Anyway, my new-to-college overachieving brain would wander during the lulls when there were no customers to ring up, and I think my department manager recognized it early on. She was awesome, and quick to let me go and do anything else when there were no customers to assist. I would head over to other departments and help restock product or fix price tags and signage in the technology sales department. I would even help to build chairs for customers as part of an additional service we offered. I was always sure to make it back to the front of the store to cash customers out when we got a little busy, but soon enough, they realized that I might be more helpful elsewhere.

And that's when I started working in the Copy and Print department. It's been called a couple of different things in it's history, but essentially this is that wonderful little corner of the store where you can print out your emails, use a copy machine, send a fax (yes, people still do that shit) or any number of other paper related projects. The funny thing is that most everyone else that worked at Paper Cuts was pretty scared of working in this department. I'm not sure if it's because you have to actually make something for a customer, or if it's because you have to remember a bunch of different item numbers, but no one ever wanted to work in that department. Being a closet crafter (remember, I was still pretty much an emo kid), I jumped at the chance to work in the Copy and Print department. For the majority of my time there, we called it DPS, so that's how I'll refer to it moving forward.

There were only three of us who knew how to run the department, which meant that most of the time only one person would be working per shift. I loved it because I genuinely enjoyed working with customers to figure out what they needed, whether it be 20 copies of a flyer or 100 spiral bound presentations. I was knowledgeable of our services, and was great at adding on binding, stapling, folding, or whatever made sense for their project. I helped to design business cards, fixed brochures and was even allowed to offer a design charge whenever I created flyer designs for a customer from scratch. I was going to school for Advertising at the time, so I felt like it was great practice for when I would have to maintain customer relationships later in life. You can go ahead and call me a nerd, I take it as a compliment.

I liked almost everything about my job. I had earned the respect of my coworkers and managers appreciated when I was working a shift with them. It was stressful and often chaotic, but I had already learned to thrive in that sort of environment so it didn't really bother me. I am one of those weirdos who seeks out chaos and then prides myself on the ability to calm things down. So, you're probably wondering what the hell this chapter is supposed to be about.

Enter Napoleon.

Napoleon was a small man if you hadn't already guessed. I don't know how tall he actually was, but if it gives you any indication, he is shorter than the infamous Napoleon Bonaparte, who was 5'2". I'm 5'2", and he was much shorter than I am. He was the Store Manager in charge of everything. And yet, he didn't have a great understanding of how to be helpful in any of the departments. He couldn't run a register, he was usually pretty unsuccessful at technology sales, and no one would dare let him near DPS. He knew how to stock product, which wasn't a huge accomplishment, and he knew how to cash out registers at the end of the night. But other than that, I don't really have any idea why he was ever promoted to the Store Manager position.

And even though Napoleon really didn't know how to run any of the departments, and he often sat in his office in the back of the store, he seemed to have this unearned ego. Possibly, it was all bravado, fueled by the bullying that he had probably received ample amounts of when he was younger due to his stature. Or maybe it was pure over compensation for his height. My honest guess? I am pretty sure that he was never allowed to be in charge when he was with his wife. I had met her on many occasions, and she was nothing but lovely to me. But when speaking with, or about Napoleon, you could almost see the scorn she had for him morph into an alien being that was ferocious and dripping with condescension. She had probably expected him to make more of himself in life and hated that he hadn't progressed any further. Who knows? I just remember hating any time that she came into the store for a visit; even more than I hated visits from corporate. After she would leave, Napoleon would be angry with everyone, and we knew it was best to avoid him at all costs. What a poor little man. I'd say that he didn't deserve it, but I really don't believe that to be true.

When I had first started, Napoleon had appreciated my work ethic and liked that I always took the initiative. The longer I worked at Paper Cuts though, the more he seemed to resent me. The longer I worked there, the more that other employees started to trust me, respect me, and confide in me. They would vent their grievances about other managers or employees to me, and I would listen and do my best to support them. Eventually, the DPS Manager decided to leave and I applied to become the new manager. I had a good understanding of how to run the department and was the most likely candidate for the job. Already I could feel that Napoleon was unhappy about my aspirations. I was still only 19 and had already earned the respect from my coworkers that he seemed to strive for. I know that if I hadn't threatened Napoleon in some way, I would have been promoted much sooner. However, after I was finally promoted, Napoleon became more and more difficult to deal with.

I stepped into my first opportunity to manage other employees and I remembered the frustrations I had experienced in my previous employment so I did my best not to perpetuate those frustrations as a boss. Stepping into my role meant that I had to replace myself in my old position and I was soon given a "volunteer" internal employee. Essentially, this means that another department didn't want him, and knowing that we had an opening, he was shuffled over to my department. I want to say that everything worked out well right from the start, but if I'm being truthful, he was terrible. We'll call him Spicoli because he just sort of was. If you're too young to know who Spicoli is, picture the guy who just says "dude" in various inflections and intonations for the majority of their responses.

In the DPS department, we were required to know how to operate at least seven different types of machines, more if you consider copy machines to be different based on their model. We were required to know how to fix them as well. If a copy machine broke down, we needed to know how to fix minor things so that we wouldn't lose business. We needed to know how to upsell or add services to copy jobs that were requested. And we needed to be able to then quickly charge a customer based on a book of item numbers that corresponded to each service and product that we sold. I'll give you an example: If a customer came into the department and wanted 20 copies of a 30-page document, it would have been our job to ask the customer what type of paper they wanted for the copies, whether or not they wanted the copies printed on one or both sides of the paper, and if they wanted it stapled or bound in some way. We would need to check if they wanted the copies to be black and white, or color, and then ask if they wanted to add covers to the project if they wanted it bound. That's the easy upselling part because all you have to do is ask. Once you and the customer had settled on what they wanted, you then had to figure out when they needed it completed. Usually, they wanted it right then and there, and you would have to handle the printing and binding while they waited. Once you finished the "job," you then had to charge them, which meant that you need to find the item number that identified each service you offered. Printing would be one item number, upgraded paper would be another, binding and covers were also separate, and the price also changed if the job was printed in color or black & white. Lots of math and item numbers still swim around in my head whenever I walk into a Paper Cuts to this day. This is all well and good if you have one patient customer to deal with. A lot of the time though, you had a line of four or five customers, and none of them were willing to wait.

For someone who is detail oriented and can multi-task by running multiple machines at once, it's a little stressful, but not impossible. For an employee who doesn't care about his job and may or may not come into work under the influence of some substance or another, it can be unimaginable. Spicoli was the latter. Whenever I spent time training him on how to do his job, I always got the very distinct impression that I was attempting to shovel through whatever haze was affecting him at the moment. He wasn't a dumb kid, he just really didn't care. He didn't ever get to work on time, and he almost always had to have others come to his aid when he was backed up with customers. This meant that sales on his shift were almost always sub-par and unacceptable. After a few weeks, I had decided that I needed to talk to him about my concerns or figure out how to get him the hell out of my department.

I remembered how Chuck had so kindly mentored me and hoped to do the same with Spicoli. And the first few times I spoke with him, he seemed to understand my concerns, but then continued to fail at his job. I eventually called him into the office for what I thought would be the final time. I was deflated and felt that I had failed at being his manager after having only been on the job for a few months.

Maybe it was because I had given up, but I decided to use that meeting to ask him why he had decided to work at Paper Cuts when it seemed like he could care less about the job. I could tell you that he was working to put himself through school or something noble like that, but he had basically been forced to get a job to continue living at home with his parents. He seemed to realize for the first time that I was frustrated with him and asked if he was going to lose his job. I was honest and told him that if he didn't improve, that we would start the process. Like I said, I didn't have a lot to lose at that point. Spicoli suddenly perked up. With his job on the line, he started to ask a ton of questions and promised that he could do better. And I realized that I had finally found a way to motivate him to do a better job. Let me stop here and let you know that I never think it is right to create an environment where hard working and high performing employees are in constant fear of losing their jobs. However, I think it is totally appropriate to be honest with an employee who is not meeting your standards and be upfront with them if they are eventually going to be let go if they do not start to improve. Spicoli taught me that it was fair, to be honest about that. He also taught me that people can change if they want to.

Through our discussion, Spicoli tried to figure out what he could do to improve. I soon understood that he wasn't trying to be an outstanding employee. He was just trying not to get fired. And we settled on the bare minimum responsibilities that he needed to do to keep his job. We wrote it out, listing each item that I would evaluate him on over the next two weeks. Through this discussion, he became very honest about the tasks that had eluded him, and we agreed that he would receive more training where needed. At the end of the discussion, we came to an agreement that he signed and dated, and I set my calendar to meeting again in two weeks. Later, as part of my graduate programs, I learned that this is almost like a performance appraisal, but at that time it was just a necessity.

I want to tell you that Spicoli miraculously improved, but that would be total horseshit. Two weeks is not enough time to change the way that a person operates. But I didn't start the process to let him go. Even though two weeks is too short for a 180-degree improvement, it is more than enough time to put forth some effort. Spicoli had finally shown some interest in keeping his job, and while he showed up late to two shifts in two weeks, that was a significant improvement from showing up late for every shift. In addition, the two times he had shown up late, he was apologetic, where previously he would have been flippant. He also spent time taking notes about how to fix the machines and process orders when he received additional training. It didn't hit every item on the list we had agreed to, but at the end of the day, that was the change that I needed to see to keep him around.

Maybe I'm just an asshole, but I think that the marked improvement in Spicoli frustrated Napoleon even more than he had been before. I don't want to seem paranoid, but it is possible that Napoleon had intentionally moved Spicoli to my department so that I would fail. When I eventually reported Spicoli's significant improvements, Napoleon seemed more annoyed than impressed, and while other managers applauded my efforts, Napoleon all but ignored them.

At some point in time, I was asked to create and manage the weekly schedule of shifts for our employees. This meant that I needed to take into account everyone's availability, the distribution of departments, and how the schedule had been handled historically. Napoleon had asked me to take over the responsibility because he said that he wanted to focus on sales when in truth, he was just terrible at it. Remembering my time with TICS, I gathered everyone's availability but also asked what shifts employees usually worked, and which ones they would prefer. I compiled their availability and put together a schedule that I felt fairly distributed shifts based on seniority and efficiency. I even listed "on-call" employees for most shifts in case the scheduled employee did not come in. It wasn't perfect the first time around, but within about three weeks, we were running a schedule that seemed to work for everyone. Knowing what seemed to work best at that point, I began asking for availability on a monthly basis and tried to distribute schedules a month in advance to give everyone a heads-up so that they could schedule their lives accordingly. Most employees were appreciative and I felt that I had done a good job.

If you haven't realized it by now, Napoleon was not happy about my success. He briefly took the scheduling responsibility away from me, telling me that he appreciated my help in the interim but that he needed it to be done "better" so he was going to handle it moving forward. At this point, I hadn't yet realized that he was threatened by my success. I was a 19-year-old kid and he was a grown ass adult. It didn't even occur to me that I was making him look bad. Not understanding his insecurities, I was disheartened when he took the schedule away from me. It wasn't until he put out his first schedule that I began to see that I was not the problem. The first weekly schedule that he posted was not available through the online employee portal, so most employees didn't even realize that he had posted it on a sheet of paper in the employee breakroom. And it was full of shifts that I knew would be empty because it didn't line up with employee availabilities. I attempted to offer suggestions but he dismissed them, and I decided not to offer up any assistance moving forward. He didn't want it because he couldn't stand to be embarrassed by a teenager. Knowing how poorly the week was likely to go, I reviewed the schedule and figured out which employees we could call to cover shifts when the scheduled employees would inevitably not be able to make it on time (or at all). I didn't share the information with Napoleon, but I did my best to let employees know if I thought they might need to be called in to help. They were frustrated with the posted schedule and appreciative of the notice. As you can imagine, the week was a bit of a disaster. Employees called in, letting us know that they wouldn't be able to make it in from their other jobs, school, or because they weren't able to get a sitter. Any shift where Napoleon was not working, I would call the on-call employee, and the shift would go smoothly. But any shift where Napoleon was working, I bit my tongue and watched him struggle to cover the empty shifts. It felt like payback, but at the expense of the other employees which left me feeling horrible.

I waited for Napoleon to ask me to handle the schedule again, but after a month, he refused to concede. Finally, I decided that I would offer to do the schedule so that he wouldn't have to deal with a bruised ego. I wouldn't have done it, except that it was significantly frustrating the employees, and I didn't want them to continue to suffer because of his over-compensating bullshit. When I offered, he quickly relented, excusing himself by saying that sales were down since he had started to do the schedule, so he guessed that I could do it again so that he could focus on improving sales. I did my best to grin and bear the tons of donkey manure this asshole was shoveling.

The final straw when it came to dealing with Napoleon came almost a year after working for him as a manager. It was time for the annual performance appraisals that were required by the corporate arm of Paper Cuts. To be perfectly honest, I was a little excited to go through the process. My performance had been appraised as a cashier, so I had an idea about what to expect. I had made some pretty significant sales improvements in the department, taken over the schedule, and surprisingly done well at retaining Spicoli. I wasn't expecting a rave review because I had felt a growing unease around Napoleon, but I had expected a fair one.

If you don't already know what a performance appraisal is (don't be embarrassed), it is basically an evaluation of you as an employee. You can be judged on subjective categories like the quality of customer service, or objective categories like year over year sales versus goals. And often at the end of the different category evaluations, the manager appraising you can provide additional comments about areas where they think you've done well or can improve. Fortunately, in the categorical sections of the performance appraisal, Napoleon had obliged and given me decent marks. Nothing to be proud of, but definitely "passing." The issue came up when he began to go into his additional comments.

Knowing the behavior that he had exhibited, and his inability to really maintain any control of the rest of his employees, I was shocked when his comments discussed my maturity level or lack thereof. He didn't have any specific examples that warranted his concern but continued to let me know that I had to be careful about how my age seemed to dictate the way that I acted around customers and other employees. I eventually found the space to interrupt and asked him if he had an example of my immature behavior so that I could work to rectify it moving forward. He let me know that it was my demeanor and that he couldn't actually pinpoint a specific behavior because it was just how I acted in general. I was heartbroken, embarrassed, and angry as all fucking hell. He was using my performance appraisal as an opportunity to cut me off at the knees, and worst of all, it had worked. I could feel the tears welling up in my eyes and asked if we could continue the appraisal later so that I could excuse myself to the restroom. I didn't wait for an answer and ran through the warehouse to the back of the store towards the bathroom.

And the story could have ended there with my overly emotional reaction, crying to myself on the disgusting bathroom floor.

But Napoleon had decided that our conversation required additional feedback, and he marched himself into the women's restroom to further explain to me that this very reaction was what he was talking about when he said that I was immature. A manager shouldn't get upset when receiving a little bit of feedback. And a manager shouldn't cry on the job. And I sure as hell should not have left my department to do so. Let's be clear here that I was not afraid for my safety, and I didn't feel like he was there to do anything inappropriate (other than badger me), but the fact is that he was in the women's restroom where I had gone specifically to get away from him.

For a few minutes, I did my best to calm down while he continued to attempt to discuss my behavior and maturity level. I tried to listen to what he had to say and to see it from his perspective. But eventually, he got to a point where he essentially told me that he had taken a chance on promoting me to the management position and that he was almost regretting that decision at this point.

In less than a year, I had taken a department that was severely underperforming regarding sales and had turned it around to the point that it was 60% above the projected sales for the year. Our department was the top in the district at the time, and it is likely that the work that I had done with Spicoli had helped to boost those sales. By this time Spicoli had finally found a part of the department that he actually enjoyed, which was fixing the machines, and he was on his way to completing his Xerox certification for machine maintenance. Additionally, based on the employee perspective, I had improved the schedule significantly in less than a month. And through all of this, I had yet to receive any customer complaints, employee grievances, or even a whisper of contention with the way that I managed my department or helped to manage the store.

All of these things ran through my head as Napoleon continued to let me know that he was disappointed in my behavior and knowing that he would not leave without some kind of response from me, I politely asked him to leave. I told him that this was the women's restroom and that he wasn't supposed to be in there. He then decided that this constituted my refusal to listen to him and complete the performance appraisal which he assured me had some very negative consequences. I let him know that I would gladly deal with the consequences if he would just get the fuck out of the bathroom. And no, I did not quietly relay this message, I yelled it at the top of my lungs.

Was this my finest moment? Of course not. Did I feel any better? Even less of a chance. Did it work? Just barely. Napoleon left, muttering his continued bullshit to himself and my heart sunk to the pit of my stomach knowing that there wasn't really any coming back from this.

You may be thinking that my adverse reaction was immature, and you are entitled to that opinion. Years later I am trying to figure out why I didn't just calm down, leave the restroom, and go on with my day. Napoleon was a small man, both in mind and stature, and I shouldn't have let anything that he said get to me. But I realize now that at the time, my perception of myself was so deeply ingrained in my success at my job that Napoleon's review was both a stab at my performance, as well as a knife right through my heart. I say that it was that way at the time, but it would continue to be for a long time after that. All of the things that I had felt I had done well had boosted my self-confidence, of which I honestly had very little outside of work, and Napoleon had effectively let me know that he didn't think anything I had done was worth shit. And because my job was so strongly bound to my personal stores of confidence, he had basically also let me know that I was not worth shit to him either.

I have no doubt in my mind that he had no idea that his actions had caused this feeling of distress. He was too much of a moron to be able to attempt to comprehend this idea. But his intention to make me look and feel horribly had worked, and I could not forgive him for it. I had no idea how to, and I knew that I wouldn't be able to accept an apology if he ever offered one up.

Fortunately, there were two other Paper Cuts in my state, and I asked for a transfer. I snatched up the first position that was available and left about a week later. A couple of months later, I was asked to help to open a new store as the DPS Manager because someone at corporate had been watching my progression from afar and was shocked when I transferred. He learned through the grapevine what had happened, deemed it inconsequential and worked to get me to sign on to the new store. I helped to open the store a couple of months later, and my department went on to outperform the other departments in the district during my time there.

So, what did Napoleon do wrong?

I thought that I would have a massive list of things that Napoleon could have improved on, but the reality is that the list is short, though heavy with items that would have been impossible for him to change. The first suggestion I would have made to Napoleon is to leave all of his personal bullshit at home. Your employees may feel sympathy for you if your wife regularly emasculates you in front of people that are supposed to respect you. They may even be on your side because she never lets you make any of the joint decisions in your marriage. However, they will not feel any of that sympathy if after they witness your wife's poor treatment, you then decide to unleash your bottled-up anger on them. Who would? Nobody likes to be mistreated because of someone else's bad day, bad marriage, or bad life.

Another thing, and hopefully you realize the trend by now, is that Napoleon had a ridiculously inflated (though unexplained) ego. And you probably think that this is a reflection on the type of boss that I prefer. You are absolutely right, but I do not think that this isn't generalizable to most other employees. Most people tend to distrust you when you take credit for things that you didn't do, you lie about how well you did on something, or you attempt to elevate yourself through self-flattery. It stands to reason that if most people don't like that in other people, that they would also dislike it in their superior at work. Napoleon's unjustified confidence seemed to stem from the ghosts of his glory days in another job, in another company; which no one at Paper Cuts cared about. He was grasping at invisible, fraying strings that would never have impressed his team anyway. And that is true for any job that you step in to. You may have been hired or promoted based on your reputation, but once you get into your new position, it is your responsibility to consistently prove how you got there.

Another major frustration with Napoleon was based on his inability to reward good behavior. This is both from personal experience, as well as the frustrations of my other coworkers. Napoleon was quick to point out how we hadn't managed a situation well or could have come to a better solution. He would dissect our errors and make sure to explain to us exactly how he would have done a better job had he been tasked with the job. Not once can I recall him taking his own advice, and often he would make similar errors to the ones that he chastised us for. He really just seemed to enjoy making us feel absolutely worthless at our jobs. You would think that someone who could surgically destroy your efforts when you failed, would also be able to determine and applaud them when you were able to accomplish something spectacular. No such luck. It's not that Napoleon couldn't appreciate us, it almost seemed like he refused to. You may think this is a harsh view of him, and that he might have been trying his best. When you are in an authoritative role, it doesn't always matter what your effort looks like. The perception that your employees and superiors are what counts and the fact that I had such a disdain for Napoleon's management style should indicate to you whether or not he was doing a good job.

It is difficult to go from a situation where you are accustomed to being rewarded for doing a good job, to then a role where you are reprimanded for even trying. At TICS and Records there was always some kind of incentive, be it tips, or free merchandise, we were always rewarded in some way for being exemplary. At Paper Cuts, there wasn't a consistent reward system. There would be times when our sales would earn our store a pizza party on a quarterly basis, but nothing else really for the rest of the year. There was nothing to drive us individually, and Napoleon couldn't even come up with an unofficial reward system. He seemed to believe in the stick instead of the carrot.

Take a minute to decide for yourself how you feel about incentives vs. punishments. Once you've decided on your perspective, consider if that is in line with how you prefer to be managed. Personally, I appreciate a balanced use of both. A threat of losing your job can sometimes be the swift kick in the ass that people need, as in dealing with Spicoli. Other times, it is important to recognize the productive accomplishments that your employees are reaching. Rewards don't have to be monetary or even based on recognition. A classmate of mine did an awesome thing and asked her employees what they would like to have as their rewards. While you will get the silly responses like "a million dollars" or "a year of vacation" you might also hear some feasible options. My classmate's employees enjoyed being able to spend time with her from a mentorship perspective, so she offered to spend an hour with them over lunch discussing anything that the employee had in mind. She enjoyed it as well because it gave her the opportunity to get to know her employees better.

Getting back to what Napoleon did wrong, the last thing that I'll bring up has to do with his restroom intrusion. Like I said earlier, I didn't feel threatened, or harassed. What was unreasonable to me was his total misunderstanding of the situation. I had excused myself from the conversation to calm myself down. He had then immediately followed me into the restroom to continue to badger me. While I know that we can't read each other's minds, there are a ton of non-verbal signals that we inadvertently release into the world when we are upset and are not ready to have calm conversations. If running to the women's restroom was not a signal that said "leave me the FUCK alone," then I need to go back to kindergarten and relearn what that looks like.

So, what should Napoleon have done differently?
Listen, I'm not saying that you always need to know the right thing to say. I'm not even saying that you need to apologize when you do something wrong. The one thing that I think everyone should work on, boss, employee, or whatever, is knowing when it is appropriate to just give someone their space and shut the hell up. A lot of the time you can get more accomplished by listening than by speaking. And in the situation with the performance appraisal, Napoleon wasn't listening to me. And I don't mean that he wasn't listening when I asked him to be excused. I mean that he was not paying attention to my non-verbal communication, which is just as important (if not more) than verbal communication. Either he wasn't listening, or he really just did not give a shit about how he was making me feel. You should never get to the point where your employee feels like they need to scream back at you to be heard. I will note that if you are in a team sport type of situation where yelling across a room to be heard over the noise of a calls for passes, go-karts, or buzzers then

you can disregard this sentiment. As an additional side note, look up Whirly Ball as a team building activity and thank me later.

What would have been appropriate in the situation with Napoleon and the women's restroom? First of all, don't fucking go into the women's restroom if your female employee has clearly gone in there to escape from you. And I am not trying to get into gender politics: Bathrooms are bathrooms, and you can pee next to me, I don't care about that. At that moment, the women's restroom was a safe place, away from Napoleon and his unfair criticisms. And the moment he breached that sanctuary, I just about lost it. Think about it this way: If your employee seems to be visually upset, with cheeks that are starting to turn bright red, pursed lips, balled up fists, and maybe even shortness of breath, maybe give them time to settle down. A lot of us need that time. I need some down time before I can re-approach an individual who has insulted me or violated my trust. It's literally human nature to avoid anything that we deem threatening. If you haven't heard of the Fight or Flight response, it is essentially our instinctual reaction to startling and sometimes threatening stimuli. Like when you go to Knott's Scary Farm at Halloween, and they pay random employees to dress up like creepy clowns and jump out at you, whatever your reaction is in that moment of fear, that's your Fight or Flight response. Unfortunately, mine is wildly unpredictable, so I am just as liable to freak out and run away as I am to sock you square in the jaw. I have to keep my hands balled up in my pockets whenever we go through haunted houses so that I don't hurt anyone.

Anyway, all I mean to say is that our reactions have evolved over time so it would be smart to pay attention to the signs, and then give your employee some space when you can tell they need it. Don't chase them into a restroom you don't belong in. Don't show up at their house when they are sick. I don't care if you don't know how to do their job, just don't do it. The good employees don't ask for enough time off. Don't make them feel like their time off doesn't actually belong to them. Sorry, another tangent, another person's story.

So, moral of that story is to pay attention to non-verbal cues, give yourself and your employees the space to settle down and be rational. And also, I don't know why I have to say this, but I'm going to say it anyway...DON'T BE SUCH A FUCKING DICK!!!!! Seriously, if people would just stop being such enormous piles of heaping shit, I wouldn't have anything to talk about.

We also previously discussed how Napoleon could have implemented some kind of unofficial reward system. Especially in jobs where your employees are doing tedious tasks or their responsibilities can be mind-numbing, cut them a break. Buy lunch for your team every once and a while. Pay for a round of drinks at the bar (underage folks excluded, obviously). Do what you can (within reason) to make their stressful jobs a little more bearable. Like I suggested earlier, you can always ask your employees what kind of reward system they would appreciate. And be consistent and fair about it. Don't just reward the employees you like, reward the employees who deserve it. Reward employees who take the initiative, who have great ideas, who lead your team in some way, who are always early or on time, who are always the last to leave. Reward your employees because they are working their asses off to do a good job to make you look good. You should realize that you need them more than they need you.

And the last thing that Napoleon could have worked on is his personal crap and accompanying ego. I don't mean to say that you need to compartmentalize your personal life and leave it with the coat guy. I am not saying that you cannot be frustrated with what you are dealing with either. I am not even saying that you shouldn't talk about it. The only thing that I would expect as a human being is to not be victimized by your personal crap. Tell me how your wife totally sucks, or that you were bullied as a kid (I'm just guessing here). I will listen emphatically and reassure you that it's not your fault. However, the moment that you make your personal problem, my work frustration, I will lose any sympathy that I would have had for you. If your wife yells at you before you leave for work and calls you a moron because you forgot to run the dishwasher, that shit is not my fault. That is between you and your wife. So, it's not okay for you to then come into work and start yelling at me, or any of your other employees for almost no apparent reason. If anything, you should have compassion for us because you are regularly being reprimanded. All you are is a bully by-product of having been bullied yourself. And your employees can tell. And they will talk shit about you behind your back. Don't give them a reason.

On a more personal note, one additional thing that I highly, and I cannot stress this enough, HIGHLY recommend that you do not do if you are a short man, is to buy yourself a humongous monster of a truck. Sure, maybe you are thinking that you look like a really tough dude when you are driving it around on the street or blasting some old 80's hair band music on the freeway. But the minute, no, the second that you have to use an additional little footstool to get out of said monster truck, you've essentially lost all of the cool points that you thought you accumulated that day. And you aren't even really impressive when you are in one of those trucks. Every time I see or hear one of those trucks drive by, the only thought that is going through my mind is "that guy must have a really small..."

So...what?: Survival Skills

Napoleon was just a man. A small, frustrated man. And before the restroom incident, there was a time that I felt like I was able to work alongside him and not want to stab forks in my ears. For me, I can't really handle it that well when someone calls me immature and won't give me space to calm down, as we've seen. I am pretty terrific at acting first and apologizing later.

This may sound incredibly stupid, and potentially like a waste of time. You are welcome to feel that way, but hear me out for a second, and then you can feel free to judge. When you work with a person who is constantly disregarding your suggestions and putting you down, you learn pretty quickly that you are wasting your breath. They aren't listening to you. All your boss is hearing is a blaring "RED ALERT! THREAT APPROACHING" every time you offer up a good idea that they didn't come up with themselves. Not all bosses obviously, but the Napoleon's of the world, definitely. So, what do you do? You can either continue to proceed as normal and lose any drive that you had to be better, or you can circumvent the system and do what you think will be beneficial.

I was fortunate enough to have other managers whom I could use as sounding boards whenever I had an idea about changing a process. We all just seemed to know better than to attempt to get final approval from Napoleon. I would vet the idea through them, make the change once we were all in agreement, and then report the results of the change to Napoleon once it was running smoothly. If you can show evidence of your success, the odds are that your Napoleon will begrudgingly allow you to continue the change you've made. Obviously, if your suggestion sucks and doesn't work out, then you should just be ready to revert back to old way of doing things. This works in a situation where you have limited supervision from your supervisor and have a little more freedom to test your ideas out.

Whatever the results of your change end up being, don't expect to be praised for your initiative or success. You won't get that from a Napoleon (or an Alice or Janice). You will earn respect from the folks that you work with though, and often that can be more important.

Another note that I will make here is something that I automatically started to do after working with Napoleon for a little while, which is that you should make it a point to second guess yourself. If you are always wondering what additional thing you missed, you will likely catch most (if not all) of them before your superior ever gets to discuss it with you. This helps on two fronts: On the one hand, you are putting out quality work that has been double checked. On the other, you are probably annoying the shit out of your egotistical boss who then has to try and figure out what else it is that you missed. I started to take it as a personal win whenever Napoleon would tell me that my suggestion was working, but that he knew something was missing. It was his way of saying that he couldn't figure out what else was wrong with it. I have to admit that it became a little fun to watch him squirm to figure out something I had missed, and then get further frustrated when he couldn't.

The last thing I will say is less relevant to my own experience, and more for anyone who is in a situation that is more extreme. I have been fortunate enough not to have been sexually harassed in any of my positions. I did not suffer the embarrassment, the lewd comments, the degrading situations, or anything even remotely related. The closest was the bathroom intrusion, which I knew was not sexually based in any way. I know that there are those of you out there who may have been in a similar situation where the intent was sexual and completely inappropriate. Let me first say that I am so extremely sorry if you are going through something like this. I wish the world were different, and please know from my perspective, you have done nothing to deserve the unwanted attention or untoward behavior. The suggestion I have for you may not heal your psychological wounds, or even quickly change your situation, but it may contribute to an eventual change. My advice is this: Document Everything. Keep a daily journal detailing the inappropriate behavior. Save all relevant emails. And encourage any of your coworkers who are experiencing the same things to also document their experiences. I can't encourage you to take voice recordings or video, because I'm not a lawyer and I can't readily say that any of that will be admissible. If you can find another job, leave and relay all of your concerns during your exit interview. If your company doesn't have exit interviews, make an appointment with your Human Resources (HR) department, and have one anyway. If you can't find another job, you should still report your concerns to your HR department. Your documentation will help, but make sure not to hand over the original copies.

Okay, getting off my soapbox now. Again, if this last paragraph is relevant to you, I'm incredibly apologetic for your circumstance and wish you a better situation in the near future.

Ask yourself, do you feel lucky?

Throughout this chapter, I ended up working with a Shitty Boss and an Asshole Employee. And maybe from their perspectives, I was the Shitty Boss or Asshole Employee. If the point hasn't been made clear to you yet, the truth of the matter is that we all have the potential to be both, and it is a matter of perception. So, ask yourself these questions and see how you stack up.

Shitty Boss:

1. How much do you think your ego plays into the way that you manage your employees? Do you ever feel threatened by an employee's demonstrated competence? Or maybe by ideas that they have offered up to the group?
2. How do you respond to employees who have proven to not only be extremely competent but also have ideas that you previously had not considered?
   a. If you tend to feel anxious and look for ways that your employee is failing, why do you think that you

search for negative aspects of your employee instead of praising their accomplishments?

b. If you usually try to incorporate new suggestions into your team, do you feel that this route has worked well for you? Do your employees seem to offer up additional suggestions?

3. How do you feel about rewards vs. punishments regarding motivating your employees?
    a. Do you favor one over the other? Which one, and why?
    b. Do you prefer a balance? Why?
4. How do you deal with your personal life when it comes to your job? Do you let it affect your day-to-day work? Do you share it with your employees/coworkers? Does that change how they perceive you?
5. When speaking with an employee who appears to be upset, how do you normally respond to them?
    a. Are you often also upset? Angry?
    b. Do you attempt to give them space?
    c. What has been a successful reconciliation attempt for you?

Asshole Employee:

1. How much do you think your ego plays into your frustrations with your boss? Do you feel the need to correct them often, especially after they have reprimanded you?
2. When dealing with a boss who seems to want you to succeed, do you feel that they are asking too much of you?
    a. How can you communicate with them regarding setting reasonable standards?
    b. How can you work to reach a compromise?
3. Do you ever feel like your maturity level plays a role in your work? If so, how?

4. How do you prefer to be motivated? And be honest, because money doesn't motivate everyone.
   a. What do you actually need from your supervisor/boss to get something done?
   b. Are you timeline driven? Or are you a little more self-reliant?
   c. How does your boss attempt to motivate you? Does it work?
5. What steps do you take to make sure that you are handling a situation professionally?
   a. Have these steps worked for you in the past?
   b. Why would you describe yourself as professional? What examples of professionalism would you provide?

Next up, we have an interesting shift away from the Bad Boss/Good Boss dynamic, and we'll talk about a boss who was a little of both. She was great in so many ways, but also sometimes a little difficult to work for. I love her to death and would work for her again in a heartbeat, but I am also honest with myself about what I needed from her as a boss.

CHAPTER 5:
The Good, the Bad, and the Learning Curve

If you've ever known anyone with any kind of cancer, or you've had it yourself, my heart goes out to you. Nobody tells you what it will be like, and very little preparation can go into dealing with it other than a strong spirit and mind. The next boss I'm going to tell you about has given me the most important opportunities of my career, and I am forever grateful to her for them. However, the opportunities often were because of the cost she was paying to fight cancer. I am going to call her Athena, because like the goddess of wisdom and war, my boss is a fighter who is wise beyond her years.

And I say 'is', because to date, she is still alive and kicking. She has literally survived death, and is a miracle embodied. She is also one of the funniest, and most amazing people that I know. If you are reading this, please accept an apology if this portrays you in a way that you feel is unfair. I can only hope to describe you in the best light possible, while being brutally honest about what employees need.

I owe Athena my livelihood and my expertise. She was kind enough and humble enough to recognize a struggling grad student who was just trying to pay rent and handed me an opportunity that would eventually grow into a career. She was appreciative of my level of competence with the "small things," and helped me provide for myself while I worked on my doctorate. Let me back up a little bit.

I started to work at the Five Pillars University (Tim, hope you don't mind that I'm borrowing this) as a graduate student worker for the Registrar's Office. I was working on my Master of Arts at the time, and just working as many jobs as I could to pay rent. I worked three jobs from 7:00 a.m. to 11:00 p.m. at night, and thankfully, I started my days working at FPU first thing in the morning. I was hired to work for Birdie, who we'll talk about in the next chapter, but quickly transitioned to help both Birdie and Athena. They seemed to recognize my ability to adapt to change quickly, as well as my attention to detail. I was appreciative of the office and the calmer pace, having only worked in retail and food service up to that point.

To make a long story short, I started off as a graduate student worker who was paid minimum wage for a maximum of 20 hours per week. I eventually was hired as a full time temporary employee and worked exclusively on running the school's graduation ceremony. I had high hopes that I would be kept as a full time employee after commencement had finished, but there were no open positions available at the time. Birdie had since moved on and recruited me to work with her at Shaman College, where I was finally a full-time employee with benefits and everything. Shaman College was affiliated with FPU and a little under a year later when Shaman College was about to shut down, I was recruited back to FPU to work for Athena still as a full-time employee. Eventually, Athena fell ill with cancer, and needed to take an extended medical leave. We'll get into the details a little more in depth later, but for now, suffice it to say that between these two amazingly strong and intelligent women, I was able to build a professional career.

The "Bad"

So, I'm going to start with the only suggestion that I would give to Athena and trust me when I say that it pains me to point this out. Athena is and likely always be a bit of a perfectionist at heart. If her name is going to be attached to a project, policy, email, or even text message, she wants to make sure that it is a point of pride as opposed to embarrassment. And because she has such a strong perspective on the quality of her work, she usually has a pretty difficult time delegating projects to her employees. You might think that this sounds absolutely amazing, right? A boss that works their ass off so that you don't have to? They do exist! And Athena is one of those people. She cared so much about the quality of the work that she produced that it was easier for her to handle projects on her own, than it was to take the time to fully explain processes to a newbie like me. And for some people, maybe this is exactly the type of job that you're looking for....well, not me.

I am one of those "special" employees that doesn't like to get bored at work. I don't always like to scour Facebook for nothing in particular while I wait to be tasked with a responsibility. My brain is kind of like a computer set on a low timer sleep setting. If I'm idle for too long, I usually just want to fall asleep at my desk. And maybe that makes me a total jerk for wanting to put in a good effort at work. I understand that is not the case for everyone, but it's always been an important part of my self-confidence at work. I appreciate the ability to self-direct and have a pretty good idea of what I should be accomplishing on a daily basis. Or even know what responsibilities are tied to which part of the year. With Athena, because she was so good at handling things on her own, I often felt like I was getting in the way or having to slowly pull off parts of the job. I was used to a fast-paced job where I was constantly being pulled in different directions and moving to a position where I had to patiently wait for a task to be delegated to me was difficult and boring.

I don't blame Athena. I totally understand why she managed the way that she did. The only suggestion that I hope to make here is to make the effort to train and delegate. It takes a lot of extra time, and you can set yourself up to have to correct more errors than you would have had to deal with, had you just completed the task yourself. But once you've trained your employee, you don't have to do that task regularly anymore, which saves you time and energy in the long run.

Another reason that I suggest learning to delegate, is so that you can set yourself to eventually leave or be promoted. If there is no one to readily replace you when you are up for a promotion, the people making the promotion decision may consider that they will just have to figure out how to fill your position next. It's not fair, but it's true. Also, if you end up leaving and you haven't trained your subordinates to handle the things that you used to handle, you are leaving them in a difficult position where they are scrambling to adjust and adapt. Maybe your intention is to screw over your people and your company, and that's definitely a relatable feeling, but you should at least realize how your actions are affecting others. I know that Athena's intentions were not to screw us over, but I remember when I was told that she would be leaving due to her battle with cancer, that I was both heartbroken and incredibly scared.

I felt like I was going to have to take on the majority of her responsibilities without ever really seeing how they fit into the full picture. By this time, she had taught me how to do a reasonable amount of the tasks, but I had never really understood how everything pieced itself together. I was about 22 when this happened and frightened that I would lose my job if I couldn't continue to hold the department together in Athena's absence. I felt like I had some pieces of a much larger puzzle, but that I was going to be judged based on the entirety of the picture instead of what I had been left with. And to make matters worse, I didn't even know what the picture was supposed to look like. I remember fighting to calm my nerves as I began to understand what my job was going to evolve into.

Before Athena went on medical leave for the first time, she developed a game plan and gave my co-worker and I the opportunity to ask her anything we were confused about. The plan was well thought out, and I was relieved, but I took the opportunity to try and fill in as many blanks as I possibly could. For those of you who don't work in academia or have never had the pleasure of working with a Registrar's Office, there are a couple of processes that we regularly manage which are cyclical in nature. For example, for every semester, we must build a schedule, get students to register for their courses, collect attendance, collect grades, and then evaluate students to make sure that they have met certain thresholds to continue attending the school. This happens every semester, generally around the same time. When we first learned that Athena was taking a leave, I knew how to complete the individual tasks like building a schedule or collecting grades, but I didn't quite understand how everything worked together. Maybe by then it was expected that I should have had an idea already, but the truth is that I had never worked in a school before, so I didn't have anything foundational to compare to, so I was constantly learning on the job.

Athena picked up on the fact that I needed to understand the bigger picture, so she helped me to develop a calendar that then detailed which tasks should occur at what time of the semester, which helped immensely. I was embarrassed to have had to ask, but thankful that she was happy to help put the pieces together. It was as if she had given me the cover to the puzzle box that showed me what the picture should look like.

When Athena eventually took her leave, I pretended that she was still there, cursing at her computer, and making light of our daily frustrations. It helped to calm my nerves whenever I worried that I was royally fucking up. I stuck to the plan, and I followed the calendar that we had developed, and I am happy to say that we fared well while she was out. The learning curve felt steep and unmanageable at times of course. Which is why delegation and cross-training are so important. But we were operating under the assumption that she would eventually return, so certain responsibilities were put on hold while she was out. She would handle them when she returned.

Eventually she came back, though her return was not permanent. Worrying that she would eventually leave again, I worked harder to fill in the gaps that I had in process and expertise. I was working against an imaginary clock to gain years of knowledge and wisdom that I couldn't even fathom, but I was desperate not to feel the worry and helplessness from her first leave. I couldn't, it wasn't possible, but I'll be damned if I didn't try.

The only point that I am trying to make here is that delegating, training, cross-training, and focusing your time and energy on preparing your employees to one day step into your position is smart on so many levels. For employees like myself who prefer to have an understanding of the bigger picture, helping them to see how different tasks and responsibilities contribute to the overall perspective can only improve their work. Most folks tend to be a little more motivated when they understand the effect that they are having on an overall process.

Let me give you an example: Let's say you've got three employees, and a task for each employee to do. You ask one employee to chop lemons in half. You ask another employee to measure a cup of sugar. And you ask your final employee to squeeze chopped lemons into water and stir. None of the employees know what you've asked the other employees to do, so they set about on their tasks. They also don't know that you are likely going to be making lemonade. What do you think would happen? Odds are, the employee who's been asked to squeeze chopped lemons into water will also find lemons to chop, because they don't know that someone else is already doing it. The cup of sugar will sit idly waiting to be added to the lemonade, and the chopped lemons will likely just pile up. Not really the best way to make lemonade, right? Consider that you tell all three of your employees what everyone's tasks are as well as let them know that your goal is to make lemonade. Which process would be more likely to produce lemonade?

Working in larger companies is not entirely different. Sure, you're not making lemonade, but odds are that everything will go a lot smoother if everyone involved has a good handle on how each step fits together. Delegating and training can help you to focus on relaying this type of information. Whenever working on new tasks, I usually want to know how it fits into the overall process. Employees appreciate context.

Another reason that it is awesome to cross-train and delegate is so that you can take a vacation and not have to worry about stepping away from your job for a couple of weeks. Athena rarely went on vacation because she was always worried that we would need something from her. And if she ever did go on vacation, because we didn't know any better, we often needed to bother her while she was away. You don't want that. You want to be able to relax on your vacation and forget about your emails and responsibilities. You can't do that if no one knows how to back you up when you are away from the office.

One last thing that I will say about cross-training and delegating is that you are not going to suddenly become easy to replace when you cross-train your employees. There is a reason that you are in a management level position, and while it may be related to tasks that you complete, it is more likely related to your level of expertise and experience. Don't be so afraid of losing your job that you get in your own way and make life miserable for yourself. Learn to delegate because at the end of the day, your employees should not be bored while you spend your entire time working your ass off. They are getting paid too, put them to work!

The "Good"

I will forever be grateful for Athena. She took the time to notice what I was capable of and then helped me to grow as a professional. I've had a lot of other supervisors who have understood that I was good at my job, but Athena seemed to know that I wanted more. She understood that I didn't plan to spend the rest of my life in a Registrar's Office, but also knew that there were still things that she could teach me while I earned my credentials and put in my dues. And I was more than willing to learn. With Athena, while it was sometimes difficult to pull tasks away from her, once I proved that I could do a good job with them, she let me manage them in full. Even though it often felt like I was working to gain her trust on important tasks, once I had her trust, she wouldn't rescind it.

Athena was also amazing at coaching us. She was so knowledgeable about what needed to be accomplished, that she would quickly be able to figure out if you had done something incorrectly. But she would never yell at you or reprimand you publicly. In fact, she would usually do exactly the opposite. If you had done something incorrectly and another department was pitching a fit about your error, Athena would publicly own up to the mistake and would never direct the blame at you. In her mind, if you made an error that eventually made it to the public, it was just as much her fault for not catching it. And if anyone disrespected you, her fiery temper was like a silver bullet with the safety off.

I remember that one of the most important things we usually had to do at the end of any semester was to collect grades from faculty members. We'd had a tough handful of semesters in the past where we had been chasing faculty down for the grades that they owed us. If we do not have grades, there are a number of other term end processes that are delayed, so it was imperative that we posted grades by the deadline. One department has been notoriously terrible at meeting the grade posting deadline, so we had decided to send out early reminders, letting the faculty and Department Chair know that the deadline was quickly approaching. I received a scathing email back from the Department Chair who thought it was extremely rude to insinuate that his faculty would not be posting their grades on time.

I was first shocked, and then extremely angry. I had never received such an undeserved admonishment from someone who was part of the problem. Sure, I had been cussed out by shitty customers before, but I guess I had believed that professionals just had better email etiquette. Let that be a lesson for any of you reading this who hasn't yet tipped your toe into the corporate world. Being a CEO, wearing a suit to work, or being a doctor who is tasked with molding the minds of tomorrow; none of it matters when it comes down to the type of person you are. People can be assholes in any and every situation, because being an asshole is not situation specific. An asshole is an asshole is an asshole.

The amazing thing about Athena is that if you were an absolute jerk to her employees, she had no fucks to give about who you were. She didn't care that this guy was the Department Chair of an academic department or that he had a doctorate. From her perspective, everyone is due a certain level of respect regardless of their years of experience or degrees. I remember going into her office after having received the nasty email, which she had been copied on, and she was livid. At first, I worried that she was angry at me, but soon realized between the fuming, cursing, and half-yelled sentences that she was upset on my behalf. She couldn't believe that he had dared to send such an email. I asked her what I should do, and she quickly calmed down and let me know that she would respond to him, and that I could move on to other things. I breathed a sigh of relief. It was like a school bully was about to get his due.

To be honest, looking back on it now, I can't recall if Athena marched herself up to his office and gave him a piece of her mind, or if she called him and ever so politely told him that if he ever sent an email like that again that she would file an HR complaint. The only thing I distinctly remember is that I knew she understood my frustrations and had done something to ensure that our department was not disrespected like that in the future. She had taken on the ferocity of a mother bear and I felt protected and very relieved to have her on my side.

Now, Athena may have had a temper fueled by justice and heroism, but she also knew when it was appropriate to release her anger out onto deserving "villains". She was more than willing to admit when she was wrong, both externally and internally within our department. She had some anxiousness that often played out in the form of micro-management, but I believe she handled her quirk beautifully. Often, when your supervisor is micro-managing you, it can feel like they are hovering over your shoulder just waiting to catch you doing something wrong. It can feel like they don't trust you, or even want you to screw up. Athena was quick to let us know that if she ever asked a question that sounded like she was second-guessing us, it was more to appease her anxieties than a reflection of the work we did. This helped immensely. On the one hand, her follow up questions always helped to remind me of steps if I had forgotten them, but I also knew that she wasn't asking them because she didn't trust me. A majority of the time, her additional questions were just quick double checks for items that I had already taken care of, but some of the time her additional questions were immensely helpful and reminded me to take care of one last thing. It was the best of both worlds. She was able to assuage her concerns, without diminishing my abilities.

Another thing that I truly loved about Athena was her ability to brazenly admit when she did not know an answer. I thought this showed an immense amount of character, and I appreciated her willingness to be humble instead of make up some ridiculous bullshit to cover the gap in her knowledge. Athena knew a LOT about our field. She understood what it took to make our department great, and she worked tirelessly to develop compliant procedures. But every once in a while, she would have to research the regulations and figure something out. And she was not afraid to do it. She was not scared to tell someone that she didn't know an answer and she would ease their concerns by letting them know that she would figure out the answer and get back to them quickly.

Having worked with bosses who had unreasonably large egos, I was so pleasantly relieved to know that Athena was not like them. She was fully aware of both her strengths and her weaknesses, and unafraid of owning both. I did not need to worry about her being threatened by my ability to learn quickly and execute well. She was understanding and accepting of her own qualities, and secure enough to want to help me instead of hinder me.

A little over a year ago, I stepped into a position that had been created explicitly for her. She had left the position years before due to her illness, but somehow I still felt extremely apologetic for taking her place. When I finally told her that I was about to be promoted into her previous role, she was overjoyed for me. She could not have been happier to hear that our company had finally given me the respect that she felt I was due. I almost melted into a puddle of tears, feeling relieved and incredibly touched by her unfailing faith in me. She is still currently fighting for her life, and she took the time to not only share in my happiness, but to be so profoundly proud of me. She is one of the most astonishing people in the world, with the most beautiful soul. I don't know what I've done to deserve a boss, and a friend like her.

So, what did Athena do right?

Most bosses wouldn't even consider doing this, but one thing that Athena did is look around for intelligence and competence and then did her best to nurture it. Instead of being afraid of grooming a replacement, she dove head first into it. She how important it is to have someone who can take over for you one day if you ever want to move up in a company. She may have had her difficulties about letting go of certain things, but it was often more due to time constraints than it was to ego or feeling threatened. If you can be secure enough to train your employees to eventually replace you, you are setting your team (and yourself) up for success.

Athena was also a force to be reckoned with. She considered many aspects of the problems that she dealt with, she was extremely knowledgeable and she stood up for what she believed in. Conflict was never a cause for her to back away from a discussion and her boldness was and is such an inspiration to me even now. I like to think that some of her strength has seeped into my bones and that I am now brave and fearless when defending what I know to be right. At least I hope so.

One of the reasons I am forever thankful for Athena was her willingness to stand up for me. I have seen it far too often where a supervisor will throw their employee under the bus and make them look bad to external constituents to avoid taking the blame themselves. I have done my best to adopt Athena's perspective that the sins of my employees are mine to bear as well. I think it is only right to acknowledge that these faults are also your own as a supervisor because you weren't supporting your employee enough to do things right.

It is even more important to stand up for your employees when they are doing things the right way. If your employee's job is to discuss regulatory requirements, and regularly tell other people that they shouldn't or aren't allowed to make-up non-compliant policies, then it is your job as their supervisor to support them 100%. I have worked in organizations where being the loudest voice in the room is more important than being the most rational, fair, or even accurate. And it's not right. But if you are a supervisor in that type of company, it is your job to be the platform for your employees to have their voices heard. The moment you fail to support them, they will lose any faith in you along with the respect that they might have previously had. Athena was unafraid of being this platform, of supporting her employees, even if she worried that her job was in danger. She knew at the end of the day that it was more important to be vocal about doing the right thing, than it was to work for a company that refused to listen to reason.

And last, but definitely not least, Athena's humility was something I wholeheartedly respect. She was unashamed of her faults and did her best to compensate for them. She was always willing to admit when she was wrong, and even more apt to figure out the right answer if she didn't already know it. As a supervisor, I still sometimes worry that my employees think I'm a total idiot because of the mistakes that I make or the dumb shit that I say. Athena may have been hard on herself about her own errors, but she never tried to hide them or pretend like they weren't her fault. (She didn't make a lot of mistakes, for the record.) She was honest about herself, and brutally so. I want to add that not everyone is born understanding what it is to be humble. And you don't have to fake the feelings of humility to gain your employees' respect. However, you should still practice the behaviors such as being honest about your mistakes and apologizing. And I mean that you will NEED TO PRACTICE, because it's not an easy habit to adopt and you will need to remind yourself. It might be difficult, but it's worth it.

I can't begin to thank Athena enough for everything she's helped me to accomplish, but hopefully she can be proud of her chapter.

What Would Athena Do? (WWAD)

We're going to discuss a few scenarios and see if you can figure out how Athena would have handled them, and then we'll go into how your actions might stack up.

Scenario 1: First Day on the Job

It's your first day at your new job and you are both anxious and excited. You have done your homework on the new company and have an idea about what might be causing issues for them. You walk into the office and introduce yourself to your new team. You have four employees who will report directly to you, and they each have very defined roles. They have all worked with the company for various amounts of time, but you are satisfied with the distribution of their responsibilities as they've explained them to you. You take a seat in your new office and are interrupted by one of your direct report's assistants. She lets you know that she can show you where you can locate your laptop and hands you a cup of coffee. You take it with two sugars, and as you lift your head to ask what she's put in the coffee, she hands over packets of sugar and cups of cream. You thankfully add in two packets of sugar as you follow her to the IT office to pick up your laptop. On the way, you ask her who she works for. She lets you know that she was recently hired full time and works for your employee who has been with the company for about a year. You ask if she's been directed to assist you, and she lets you know that when she started she had to figure out a lot of this stuff on her own, so she's taken it upon herself to help out. Her supervisor has given her permission, as he often doesn't have much for her to do anyway. The two of you obtain your laptop, she makes a brief stop to show you where the coffee is, and you head back to your office. She lets you know where she sits if you ever need anything else and disappears behind a cubicle wall. Knowing that it's your first day, what ideas are brewing in your mind?

1. You've met your team, and they all have specific responsibilities. You can see that while they have a detailed understanding of their own positions, that they don't necessarily know how everything works together.
    a. What ideas do you have concerning your team? Do you let them continue as is? Do you take some time to get the lay of the land first? Why?
    b. You want to get to know your team a little better. How would you approach it?
2. You look into the structure of the department and realize that all of your direct reports have at least one assistant to help them with their day to day tasks. You know that one assistant has made a good impression on you.
    a. Are you considering reorganizing the department? Why?
    b. What is your timeline for change?
    c. What would be your timeline for training?

Scenario 2: Change Management

You've been working at the company now for about a year. You've realized pretty early on that one of your direct reports is competent but really doesn't enjoy his work. He is interested in working for another department in the company and appears to be biding his time. He also happens to be the supervisor for the assistant who was so helpful to you on your first day. You are considering making a structural change to the department that will involve cross-training for your direct reports and their assistants, but you aren't quite sure of the best way to go about handling it. You have a private meeting with your direct reports to get their input, and they seem hesitant to make changes to their current way of doing things. How would you handle it?

1. You speak with the external department, where you know your current employee will be an asset, and they will not be able to hire any additional employees for another nine months. You bring your employee into your office and let him know that you have a feeling that his interests are external to the department, and that while you would love to retain him, you also want to set him up to enjoy his professional career. He seems shocked at first, but then thankful. You let him know that you've spoken to the external department, but that they aren't quite ready to hire. What do you do next?
    a. Do you let your employee continue to do his job as is? Do you provide him with opportunities to collaborate with the external department? How? Why?
    b. How do you plan to support his current position when he does eventually leave?
2. Your employees are concerned about the potential change, but have trouble pinpointing their exact issues. You guess that they are fearful that the change will make their jobs more stressful or that they will appear less competent. What would you say to them?
    a. Are there any benefits that you can discuss regarding cross-training and delegating?
    b. Can you come up with a game plan that will put their minds at ease?

Final Thoughts

For some of you, the thought of helping an employee to leave your department may seem ridiculous. Or including your employees in the change management process many seem like an unnecessary step. If that's the case, you should probably re-read the first couple of chapters, because you've haven't figured out yet that it's beyond important to have a team that is responsive to change in a productive way as well as a team that is invested in continuing to do a good job. There is nothing wrong with an employee who does a good job but doesn't ultimately want to end up in your field. They'll appreciate you if you work with them to prepare them for their next job. And their quality of work will not drop off in the meantime. So, why not invest a little extra time and have a candid conversation with them?

The next chapter is about a lovely woman who gave me a chance based on a phone interview and continued to send opportunities my way over and over again. As with Athena, I am indebted to Birdie and cannot thank her enough for believing in me. We're going to rewind a bit and talk about how I even got the job working with Athena. Bear with me.

CHAPTER 6:
Everything You Ever Wanted, Even for a Moment

After I finished undergrad, I took a semester off to figure out what I wanted to do next. I had double majored in Psychology and Advertising, but I didn't feel a strong pull to work in either field alone. I knew that I did not want to continue to study Psychology from a clinical perspective. I didn't have the patience or "bed-side manner" to do the job, and on a more personal level, I really just didn't think that I would be able to handle the onslaught of other people's emotions when I was just learning how to deal with my own. That's another story for another book completely. I knew that I enjoyed being creative but hated being bound to the expectations of clients, so I decided to forego pursuing Advertising as a career.

In my last semester of undergrad, I had fortunately stumbled onto Industrial/Organizational Psychology which is basically the study of people at work. By that time, I'd been working for about five years and brash young asshole that I was, I thought I could get into a field where I told other bosses how to do a better job. I've really never stopped thinking that, so I guess I'm still a brash asshole, I'm just not as young anymore.

Anyway, I'd fallen into nerd heaven and was set on focusing on I/O Psych. At the time, none of the schools on my little island home offered such a program, and I was excited to finally venture off the "rock". (For those of you who have never lived in Hawaii for an extended period of time, it can get entirely too small, so locals will sometimes refer to their home island as the "rock" to reference both its size and volcanic beginning.) By the time I had figured out what I wanted to do, I was a little late for the Fall enrollment period, so I had resolved myself to take a semester off and apply for the Spring. Anxious as I was to get started, I decided to attend the school that had Spring enrollment options and was willing to accept me in January. I didn't want to waste any more time.

I moved to California to start my program, equipped with a small savings fund and my retail experience. I thought I was going to kick some ass with my "years of experience". I started my master's program and was bored out of my mind. This is not a reflection of the program. It is just that it was set up for working professionals and I had no job to speak of so I didn't know how to contribute to discussions. For the first two months, I slept in 'til 2:00 p.m., stayed up until 3 a.m., and was living in a sort of secluded area without a car and I relied heavily on my roommate for rides just to get out of the apartment. Thank you, Cherise. I swear you saved my life.

I quickly figured out that I needed some kind of job to support myself (my scholarship was running low) and to bring some sanity back into my life. I used my savings to get a car and found the nearest Paper Cuts to see about a transfer. In the same week, being nervous about the transfer not going through, I randomly applied to work for the Department Chair of my program at school. I had interviewed with her and was extremely impressed and in awe. I was sure that she was who I wanted to be when I grew up, and I thought it might be a good idea to hopefully let some of her awesome unicorn dust rub off on me.

Birdie was quick to ask me to set up a phone interview and I remember not understanding what a phone interview was. I probably should have thought about it a little more formally, but I ended up taking the interview in my pajamas, on my bed at home, hoping that I wasn't embarrassing myself. Maybe I was the only one who applied, maybe her previous retail experience helped her to recognize the value of mine. I've never asked for fear of her answer, but regardless she let me know that I had the job, but that it had changed slightly.

The job description had indicated that I would be her assistant, and at the time that it was posted she was the Department Chair of my program. Since the posting, she had also been hired to be the Director of Student Services and she seemed to think that I would be a good fit to assist her with that job. I had no idea what that entailed, I was just happy to be employed. Shortly after that, I heard back that I would also be starting to work at Paper Cuts again, so I went from having no source of income to having two in less than a week. I'd balanced working full time and going to school in undergrad, and in my grad program I was on campus even less, so I figured that working two part-time jobs wouldn't be as strenuous. I wasn't right, but I managed.

I'd been hired on specifically to assist with a project to audit all student files. Five Pillars University (FPU) had just acquired another school and Birdie had been tasked with the records transition. Athena hadn't yet been hired, so Birdie relied on myself and my coworker to audit hundreds of files. Hundreds of musty, falling apart, sneeze inducing files. It was boring, but it was calm, and I was happy to sit at a desk when the alternative meant running around Paper Cuts helping rude customers.

It seemed like it took forever, but eventually the project was done. Somewhere along the line Athena was hired, and I transitioned to helping her. And eventually, Birdie moved back to the mid-west. Birdie steps back into the picture when I was right about at my wits ends with trying to find a full-time job with FPU. I felt that I had put in my dues and was ready to stop working multiple part-time jobs to make ends meet. The FPU position I had applied for was given to someone else and while the role I had applied for had changed and I knew that I was no longer appropriate for it, I was devastated.

Birdie happened to give me a call around that time and let me know that she needed to hire a Student Advisor. She'd been hired to be the Director of Student Services at Shaman University and she wanted to work with someone that she could trust because she would be working remotely from the Midwest, but the school was located in Santa Barbara, California. I jumped...no...leaped at the chance to work for Birdie again and set about preparing for the interview. Santa Barbara was about two-hours north of me, but I didn't particularly care if it meant that I could finally settle down a bit and have a "real job". I drove up for the interview with the President of the school about a week later and was offered the job while I drove home. I was elated and accepted immediately.

So, what did Birdie do right?

Working for Birdie again was awesome. She is sort of everything that you don't even realize that you want in a boss. She knows what she's doing, but also knows how to manage others. Not everyone can do both. Birdie seemed to innately understand what her employees would need from her and worked hard to be that type of boss. She trusted me to do a good job, but also was able to coach me in a sensitive and fair way whenever I needed it. I received regular feedback from her and she was always honest. Because Birdie had been my Department Chair, she also understood the career trajectory that I eventually hoped to take and she worked to include the elements of that path into my projects and responsibilities.

While at Shaman University, I also needed to audit student records and I wasn't looking forward to it. Birdie seemed to know and understand the apprehension, and regularly scheduled check-in meetings so that I could report on my projects. This kept me on task and eliminated any potential for procrastination. I appreciated the structure without any implied distrust. She knew what I needed and did it.

Working remotely, Birdie also gave me a lot of space to manage myself. She gave me suggestions for when different tasks should be completed, but didn't micromanage me. I want to point out that this is particularly impressive because of the fact that Birdie worked remotely. When you put a large physical distance between a supervisor and an employee, there is a tendency for distrust to build. Because your boss can't see what you are doing, they may wonder if you are doing anything at all. It's a totally understandable worry because most people believe that if they were to work remotely, that they wouldn't be able to motivate themselves to do their jobs. I've been working remotely for the past five years and still find it difficult sometimes. Despite those odds, Birdie trusted me. The distance didn't seem to worry her, and she didn't question my work ethic or integrity. We had obviously had the opportunity to build that trust over a short amount of time previously, but it is so easy to forget that kind of history. It could have very easily evolved into an environment of anxiety and constant updates, but Birdie never let it get anywhere close to that.

Like Athena, what I appreciated about Birdie was her willingness and ability to support me from a professional and personal standpoint. Not only did she help me to finally transition to a full-time position, but then she helped to make sure that the position would be worthwhile for me based on what she knew I had planned to do in the future. She was able to manage me as a person, instead of a job description, and it's something that is severely lacking in a lot of managers.

Birdie also always kept an eye out for opportunities to praise and reward her employees, even if it was for unrelated talents. For example, as an Advertising major in undergrad, I had created logo's and used different design software for mock-up advertisements. Once Birdie learned about my additional skill, she actually asked me to create a logo for her. For some people, this might seem like something that is not part of the job description, that I shouldn't have been asked to do. But for me, it was acknowledgement that Birdie could appreciate me as a whole person with unique talents and abilities. And not only did she appreciate me for it, but she trusted me enough to utilize those talents.

When we were back at FPU, Birdie had also found out that my classmate and I spent some of our weekends messing around with low quality music recordings. We recorded our covers of popular songs and shared them with our friends and family. Birdie happened upon one of these recordings, listened to it, and then decided that I should sing the National Anthem at our inaugural commencement ceremony. Externally, I was terrified because I feel physically ill whenever I am asked to perform in public. But internally, a tiny part of me was extremely proud. Scared as shit, but proud as hell.

And Birdie is like that. She always wants to build you up so that you feel confident and proud of yourself both as an employee and also as a person in general. I didn't know that I was looking for someone to accept me so fully, until I worked for Birdie, and I am so thankful for having had the opportunity.

Did it Work?

I didn't work at Shaman University for very long, because the school was shut down not long after I arrived due to accreditation issues. Because of that it's hard for me to say whether or not Birdie's management style had a particular effect on productivity or efficiency or anything like that. What I will say is that if Birdie were ever to offer me a job again in the future, I would most likely take the job. Even if it meant a pay cut or a step down in title. Working for a good boss can be so much more important for your overall personal well-being and job satisfaction. I might not move to the mid-west, because I can't really handle the cold weather, but I would still consider making the change for her.

Now that I'm thinking about it, even though I don't work for Birdie anymore, I would still do pretty much anything for her. I probably wouldn't help her bury a dead body, but I wouldn't do that for anyone really. However, if she asked me to put together an excel spreadsheet that detailed how many times the word "stapler" is mentioned in Office Space, I would do it. I might look at her quizzically and think that she is a weirdo, but I would do it, because she means that much to me. And you want to be a boss that can evoke that kind of response from your employees. I better get to work on that spreadsheet. Office Space isn't going to watch itself. (I'm totally kidding, but now I do want to go and re-watch Office Space.)

What Would Birdie Do? (WWBD)

Time for another fun scenario. I'll make it easy on you, and just write up a short and simple one. If you've been paying attention the answer should be glaring back at you if you even skimmed this chapter. Ready?

Scenario: Employee Relations

You've just completed the interview process to fill an empty spot on your team. You have two seasoned employees and believe you have just found your third. You offer him the position, and he starts two weeks later. You sit him down on his first day, offering him coffee and letting him know that you are excited to have him. He look's nervous and fidgety, so you do your best to put him at ease. What do you discuss with him during this meeting?

1. If you've decided to discuss his job responsibilities, he's started to calm down a bit, but also seems to have glazed over. While he will likely be great at this job, you consider

that it is not what he is truly passionate about, what do you do?

2. If you've decided to ask him more about himself before going into job responsibilities directly, he's mentioned that he surfs on the weekends and is highly involved in a non-profit organization that teaches kids how to surf. How does it help you to know this information?

Final Thoughts

Like I said, just one short and sweet scenario. Hopefully, you've figured out that it's important to understand the employee as a person, and that knowing what they enjoy doing on their off days can help you to build rapport and start a respectful, professional relationship. If you're a CEO, you may not have the time to have this kind of relationship with every single one of your employees. Which is fair, because your company may be huge. But it's important to understand that this should be modeled to your direct reports, who should then model it to their direct reports. If you build a company based on treating your employees with human decency and general kindness, you can promote job satisfaction, and decrease turnover. People aren't going to want to leave if they feel like they are being cared for or feel that they are being treated fairly. People don't tend to leave jobs where they feel safe.

The next chapter is about a couple of terrible bosses whose stories so closely intertwine that it didn't make any sense to split them up. I'll give you a fair warning that I am still fairly frustrated and angry about this situation, so please excuse the swearing and hopefully not too slanderous descriptions of them.

CHAPTER 7:
Spineless and Ridiculous

At 25, I was working through my doctoral program at FPU while I also held the Assistant Registrar position. We skipped around a little bit, so to remind you, I had worked with Athena, and she had prepared me to handle a good amount of the Registrar responsibilities while she was out on leave. At this point in my career, she had returned and then accepted a role working for the UB Corporation where she helped to support Registrar Offices at two other schools along with FPU. We'll talk a little more about the UB Corporation in the next chapter, but you can think of it as a shared services organization that helps to provide expertise and services to smaller schools. It's kind of like outsourcing, but instead of outsourcing call center jobs, you are outsourcing services related to Financial Aid, Regulatory and Compliance Risk Assessments, and Records Management. Athena specialized in records and regulations and was able to share her expertise to support other schools along with FPU.

For a while, FPU didn't really work that hard to replace Athena, and the Registrar role was left unfilled. Being only 25, I didn't really think that I was equipped for the role and felt that I lacked the years of experience that would have helped me to be ready to be the Registrar. So I didn't apply for the role and remained in my Assistant Registrar position, while I still ended up taking over a good amount of the responsibilities of the Registrar. This also left me reporting to a director whose focus had mainly been on students, instead of regulatory requirements. The difficulty that I have with this part of my career is that at first, I really did appreciate working with her. We'll call her Lucy. To give you an idea of the department structure, Athena originally reported to Lucy, and then my coworker and I reported to Athena. When

Athena went on medical leave, and then eventually left altogether, my coworker and I reported directly to Lucy, and this was fine for the most part. Lucy didn't know how to use the student records software so she couldn't really help to back us up during peak times, but she also seemed to trust us enough to handle the day to day responsibilities. She didn't micromanage us and seemed like a genuinely caring person. I grew to trust Lucy and felt like I could express my concerns without fear or reprimand. To her credit, she did try to manage us by having regular check-in meetings, even if she couldn't always help us with the issues that concerned us.

Now, FPU is a school with multiple campuses, with redundant roles that focus on the campus specific student populations. I supported the California student population, while we had two additional Registrars to support our other campuses. As is likely to occur when this sort of redundancy exists, procedures begin to become distinct and disagreements over the best way to manage a situation can arise. We needed a unifying leader, and the powers that be at FPU decided that instead of filling Athena's role, they would use the position to hire a university Registrar. Under Lucy's direction, the Registrar's and I set about searching for a candidate, and eventually decided to hire Derek. He had a great resume, interviewed well, and seemed to have the attitude that we needed to make the necessary changes to improve our department both from an efficiency and compliance perspective. I was excited for him to start because while Lucy had been a great boss in the interim, I thought working with Derek would give me the opportunity to expand my knowledge base on how to be a Registrar. It's a good thing I didn't bet any money on that potential growth.

Derek started in January, and like Athena, he reported to Lucy, while we reported to him. At first, it seemed like Derek was going to work on the improvements that we desperately needed. He called a meeting to ask us what we considered to be our biggest concerns and how we felt the department could improve. We shared our perspectives and provided specific areas that we hoped to focus on. Derek listened intently and took notes. I was elated!!! We were finally going to get the support that we needed, with the professional experience to defend the initiatives. Or so we thought.

In February, Derek had decided to focus on making changes to student transcripts and change them from a landscape format to a portrait format. And no, that had not been on our list of suggested improvements. We honestly didn't know where the idea had come from. He let us know that it would save the school a lot of money and seemed to focus all of his energy on the project. I still had hope that he had chosen the transcript "improvements" as an initial starter project to get a good understanding of how the school operated. Go for the low hanging fruit as they say. I tried to wait patiently as he spent a majority of his time in the office on the phone with his mobile phone provider, attempting to fix his personal phone service. I attempted to ignore the loud conversations that he had with people he described as his former consulting clients. I pretended that he was in the office when he often decided to "work from home".

At this time, the Registrar for one of the other smaller campuses was let go, and it was decided that I would take on her responsibilities. I was out sick the day that they let her go, and I was notified by my coworker of the significant change. Keep in mind that when this happened, I was still only employed as an Assistant Registrar, which is basically two structural tiers below a Registrar. With one Registrar gone, we still had one remaining Registrar from the other campus, as well as Derek as the University Registrar to choose from. Now, I don't really know if it would have been fair for the other Registrar to support the vacancy, but I absolutely believe that Derek could have supported the role as he seemed to be doing nothing else but bitching about a transcript that nobody seemed to care about.

I remember when my coworker called me. I was feverish and curled up in bed. Ever the anxious worrier that I am, I immediately picked up the phone when I saw who was calling. When he told me of the change, I seriously wondered if I was hallucinating. He had wanted to give me a heads up before I came back to work so that I knew what to expect. While he would also have to help with the transition, he and I both knew that I would be handling a majority of the responsibilities.

Taking on a new campus of students, small population or not, is an endeavor that takes a lot of communication and relationship building. And to make things even more difficult, the campus was located on the other side of the country, a three-hour time zone difference. I looked to Derek and Lucy for some direction on how to handle the transition. Neither of them had any suggestions. Lucy didn't quite know what needed to be transitioned, and Derek just couldn't be bothered. I set to work reaching out to the Dean of the campus, hoping to start there to begin supporting the new campus.

I held a virtual meet and greet, introducing myself and letting everyone know how I hoped to support them. I asked them to try to be patient with me as we worked through the transition together, and then quickly began to have one on one meetings with the Department Chairs for each of the academic departments. They seemed to appreciate the dedicated support that they apparently had not been receiving before, and I felt solace in the fact that I had at least made some positive strides forward for these neglected academic programs. Even through my frustration with the unfair addition of responsibilities (and no, of course they didn't give me a raise), I seemed to have made the best of a shitty situation.

In March, Derek had still not made any of the suggested improvements and was still only focused on the transcript project. And his unprofessional office behavior did not subside. On a daily basis, I remember getting up from my cubicle desk to shut his office door so that I wouldn't have to hear him yell at his phone provider. I appreciated the days when he wasn't in the office, because at least we had some peace and quiet. And by this time, Derek had started to grow rude and aggressive in emails. He would be visibly angry and frustrated at the UB Corporation employees (namely Athena) because they held the access to the student records software, that he felt he should have. Derek had also failed to make any moves to replace the Registrar who had been let go. I had taken on the additional campus with the understanding that it would be a temporary resolution. But just as the school had taken forever to replace Athena, it also seemed like they wouldn't work any more quickly this time around. I began to become more and more frustrated with the whole situation.

In April, there were still no improvements and I considered consulting with Lucy, who I felt I could trust. I decided that a couple of months might not be enough time to begin to focus on the improvements we had suggested and tried to excuse his behavior. Eventually after no improvement, I asked Lucy if I could speak with her and she welcomed me into her office. I expressed my concerns with the lack of improvements, the disruptive outbursts that came from his office, the additional campus of students, and the reality that we could hear him discussing contracts that he still maintained with his "former" clients. Lucy listened and tried to be understanding of my concerns. Because of his temper, I asked Lucy not to let him know that the concerns were coming from me specifically. She agreed and I stupidly believed her.

In May, Derek seemed to be even angrier and less productive. He showed up less and less. I let Lucy know that my concerns persisted, and shortly after that Derek called me into his office. Up until this point, Derek hadn't done anything that was aggressively directed at me. His inaction was negligent, and his failure to support the vacant Registrar role seemed lazy and fucking annoying, but he generally seemed fine to let us handle our daily responsibilities as long as we didn't bother him. When he called me into his office, I realized pretty immediately that I now had a bright, flaming red target painted on my forehead and knew that only Lucy could have supplied the darts. I fumed silently, fists balled up in my lap, mentally kicking myself for trusting her.

Every concern that I had shared with Lucy spilled out on to his desk like sharp, angry shards of hate. Who was I to dictate to HIM what the focus of improvements should be? How dare I try to say that he should be managing the vacant Registrar role! He let me know that I had no idea what it was like to be in his position, and that I couldn't just go over his head to Lucy whenever I didn't like the way that he was doing things. And part of me understood that. I should have discussed my concerns with him directly, but the truth is that at the time I thought he was absolutely insane, and I was scared of him. I didn't tell him any of this. I sat there, trying to figure out how to end the conversation. I didn't agree with any of his explanations, but any attempt to dispute them was immediately interrupted. If I wasn't there to comply and agree with him, I was going to continue to be hassled. I decided to feed his bullshit back to him as convincingly as possible just so that I could leave. I was tired of getting yelled at and so terribly disappointed by Lucy's part in it.

Maybe Lucy had thought that she was doing the right thing by letting Derek know of my concerns. Maybe she thought that Derek was a reasonable person who wouldn't retaliate in such a hostile manner. Maybe she thought that Derek would try to understand and adjust his improvements and behavior. Maybe she was just totally fucking wrong about everything that she expected of Derek, and I was the one lined up to pay in full for her error in judgment. Any previous feelings of trust and respect that I had for Lucy vanished. She had betrayed me and I felt like I was being fed to a rabid dog. For a moment, I was hurt, and then fiercely angry. Not only had her actions failed to improve the situation, they had in fact made it unquestionably worse.

I felt numb, as I thought I had expressed valid concerns to a reasonable person and was met with an explosion of fury and rage. I wasn't scared of him anymore, though. I loathed him, but I wasn't afraid. What else could he do? It definitely couldn't get any worse, right? Wrong.

At the end of May, over the Memorial Day weekend, I received a vile email that literally still gives me acid reflux every time I read it. Up until this point, I had a pretty spotless track record. Faculty and staff alike respected me and looked to me as a resource. They trusted me to do a good job, and generally expressed appreciation for the effort that I put into the work I did. Even the campus that I had been "voluntold" to support had positive feedback for me.

I had taken the Friday before Memorial Day weekend off to spend with my then boyfriend (now husband) to celebrate his birthday. I had requested the day off in advance, reminded Derek and my coworkers that I would be out and was relieved on Thursday afternoon to have a nice little reprieve from work. On Friday (when I was already gone for the week) I received an email asking me why a project had not yet been completed. The email explained to me that a project this important needed to be a priority over requested days off or weekends or holidays. It further detailed to me that I should continue to work on the project through the holiday weekend in order to have it completed by the following Tuesday when we returned.

The first thing you should know is that I didn't read that email until Monday night, so I had a nice long weekend, happy not to have to deal with Derek. (Thank God!) The second thing, is that while the project had an explicit deadline, that deadline had never been communicated to me by Derek or anyone. And the last thing you should know is that even though that deadline had never been communicated to me, Derek saw fit to copy a number of different high ranking employees on this nasty email which included both Lucy, and FPU's President. The fucking school president. He didn't just set me up to fail and throw me under the bus. He got out of the bus, laughed at my mangled up body and then got back in the bus and ran me over again. Who the fuck does that?!

I was distraught, because even though I had not been told of the deadline, I was sure that I was going to be fired. My spotless record felt like it had been smeared with vile streaks of shit and vomit, and no amount of bleach would be able to clear my name.

And then, I was angry: Furious, white hot, blood boiling angry. This is definitely where you can tell that I am a millennial, and I'm pretty much okay with that.

The Tuesday that I returned from the holiday weekend, I sat quietly in my cubicle and drafted a short and simple resignation letter. I knew it meant that I would be jobless for the first time in almost ten years, and I just didn't fucking care. I refused to be mistreated in such a horrific manner, based purely on principle (see, millennial). I would not stand for it, and I didn't care if it meant that I had to go back to working at Paper Cuts or be unemployed for a little while. I believed that anything was better than working for Derek while I continued to feel unsupported and betrayed by Lucy. (Years later in a related situation, I'm happy to say that I didn't throw up my hands, shout "Fuck You" from the rooftops and quit...though I was pretty close.)

Derek didn't come back to work in the office after he received my resignation. He didn't contact me at all. And I was fine with that. FPU's president asked Human Resources to talk to me to try to get me to stay. I remember the HR Director asking me if they would be able to increase my salary to encourage me to reconsider. I let him know that no amount of money would cause me to reconsider. When he asked what he could do to change my mind, I let him know that unless he was willing to make an immediate personnel change, namely firing Derek, there was no way that I would stick around. He looked shocked, quickly jotted down my response and thanked me for my time.

Lucy spoke to me on my last day and told me that it was unfortunate that I was letting a difference in personality drive my decision. I let her know that I felt her idea of a difference in personality was a poor description of the situation. I told her that if this were truly a difference in personality, I would be the only person leaving. The reality is that once I put in my resignation, my coworker resigned a week later. And the only remaining Registrar decided to step down into a different role. Derek was like an infectious disease worming his way through the organization and I was happy not to be sick anymore. I left the day before I turned 26, because Fuck You if you think I was going to spend my birthday working for that asshole.

And maybe you now have the impression that I'm extremely irrational and immature. In hindsight, I was. But I also consider my response to be responsible in two respects. The first being that I knew if I were to stay on for much longer that I would not have continued to be professional, so they would have fired me eventually. The second is that while I struggled for a couple of months to find another job, and I grappled with who I am without a career, for the first time in five months I felt like I could breathe. And I will take the ability to breathe over appearing rational any day.

Whenever you leave a job that you detest, most of us will get just a little happier than we should when we hear that our replacement sucks, or that the company can't survive without us. It's childish, but I am not immune to that feeling and was always delighted to hear how Derek was driving the department into the ground. Scratch that, he didn't just drive the department into the ground, he crashed it into the planet's core like an errant asteroid with no aim, direction, or intelligence to speak of. My replacement was a graduate student worker whose inability to recognize her own faults coupled with her desperate desire to please everyone, was the perfect dish of revenge that I didn't even have to serve up on my own. As the story goes, once my coworker and I had left, Derek stuck his head out of his office, pointed at the nearest student worker and asked her if she wanted to be the new Assistant Registrar. I didn't feel betrayed in the least when she jumped at the opportunity because she belonged to another part of the department, and she was terrible. I was vindicated and was happy to see that not just anyone could replace me.

Eventually, someone at FPU finally realized what an absolute monster Derek was, and they finally fired him in October of that same year. By then I had a new role, having followed Athena to work for the UB Corporation and Lucy reached out to me to see if I would consider coming back to FPU to become a Registrar. I politely declined. While the position would have meant more money and a more impressive title, I knew that I could never trust Lucy again. I knew that I would constantly be second guessing her actions and never feel safe working for her. Give me a boss who I can respect and trust, who in turn, also respects and trusts me, and I will never leave. Force me to work for a boss that never backs me up, constantly throws me under the bus, or belittles me, and you won't even hear me head for the door. I'll already be on the other side figuring out my next steps.

So, what did Lucy and Derek do wrong?

I'll start with Lucy because my grievances with her are short and sweet. Lucy did not have a lot of expertise in our area, which often made it difficult for her to support us. From a practical standpoint, this is just a difficult situation to put yourself in as a boss. If you don't have at least a preliminary understanding of what your employees deal with, it is likely that you will sound like an idiot when you try to help them. And don't try to kid yourself, employees can always tell when they know more than their boss about a specific topic, so don't try to fake it. If you don't know what you're talking about, just be honest, and help them in whatever way that you can. Like I have said previously, your employees will appreciate the honesty. They also tend to appreciate it when they can tell that you are make a concerted effort to actually try to understand their area of expertise. If you ask them for additional perspective or clarify a point to make sure that you are understanding the situation, they are likely to even try to help you learn. Lucy actually did a pretty good job of this. She was honest that she didn't understand a lot about the software system that we used, so I appreciated it whenever she was trying to figure something out. It's not impossible to manage people if you don't have aligned areas of expertise, but it can be difficult if you don't put forth any effort to acclimate yourself to the new subject matter.

Probably my biggest grievance against Lucy was her decision not to support me once I was no longer her direct report. It felt as if she had decided that because Derek was now my boss, that she shouldn't have to worry about my concerns. And maybe that's true from a structural perspective, but from a relational viewpoint, it doesn't send a positive message to previous subordinates. I had thought that I had developed a strong working relationship with Lucy, and that she respected me and cared for my well-being, the same way that I did for her. And maybe she did, but her actions failed to support this notion. And even though it's a cliché, actions absolutely speak louder than words. You can say that you are willing to take a bullet for someone, but when it comes down to it, are you really? And while words can be a kind consolation prize, they are in no way a replacement for the steadfast rigidity of actions.

Moving on to Derek, there are obviously numerous areas where he could have improved. We'll start with his inability to know the appropriate time and place. For example, there is a very specific time and place for work, and for most people that is between 9:00 a.m. and 5:00 p.m., Monday through Friday, in an office somewhere. For Derek, these were loose recommendations that he felt did not apply to him directly. He was allowed to show up late, leave early, or sometimes fail to show up all together. For remote employees, I understand that this is different, and that you have the flexibility to manage your time as you see fit. Derek was not a remote employee, or if he was, that had never been explained explicitly to us. From my perspective, he just didn't care because no one was reprimanding him for it. Derek also didn't seem to understand that the time and place to deal with non-work related issues was not when he was supposed to be at work. He would regularly berate his poor cellphone provider while he was in his office, and the volume was at such a high level that we could hear his conversations straight through the wall without even trying. Most of the time he would actually leave his door wide open so that we had to deal with his open hostility about something that was not even work related. I would often try to politely shut his door but regardless, his temper would not be contained.

I'm not going to tell you keep your non-work responsibilities at home. I feel like it's fair to assume that because we spend so much time at work that you are going to run into situations where your non-work responsibilities creep into your work day. What I will say is Derek needed to do a MUCH better job of hiding that shit from the rest of us. Go ahead, have your asshole conversation with your phone provider. Scream at them and tell them that they are complete idiots who have no right to work in a technology-related industry (I'm paraphrasing). But do that shit away from your office or shut your goddamn door!!!!! Seriously?! Why is this something that even needs to be said? Not only did Derek do an AMAZING job of belittling the poor customer service rep that he was speaking to, but he also communicated to us that he could and would absolutely speak to us accordingly. In the same breath, his decision not to hide his hateful conversations felt like utter disrespect. When you share walls with your employees, and you know that they have regular conversations with consumers (in our case, students), don't raise your voice if you can help it. You are making yourself look like a total jackass to your employees, and the people that they are working with. And if you become known for having conversations at volume 11 on a regular basis, trust me when I tell you that word gets around.

Derek also gave us the very real impression that he did not give a shit about how we felt. Our opinions did not matter, and he was going to do whatever he wanted to do. I can respect this feeling at some points, but if you're going to be this kind of a dictator, you should just own it. Don't try to get our input and then just completely ignore it. That makes it even more frustrating, because you've then inadvertently given us hope for no reason.

Not only did Derek not care what we had to say, but he also seemed to reject our concerns. He wasn't going to help us with any of the changes that we wanted to work on, and instead he would dump additional responsibilities on us. He appeared to want to get paid a fuck ton of money to do absolutely nothing but bitch to his cell phone provider and harass employees. Great, thanks for that.

While I can understand that most individuals would like to get paid to do nothing, the basis of my frustration here is the selfishness of the way that he did everything. Maybe it's because I'm the oldest of four kids, or maybe it's because I come from a naturally collectivistic culture, but it has always been engrained in me that the needs of the many outweigh the needs of the few. There is a time and place for being selfish, and it is not when you are supposed to be managing employees. Being a good manager is about understanding the needs of your employees, and then figuring out how to meet those needs. Obviously, within reason. We can't give all of our employees a million dollars, ask as they might. But we can give them our time, our concern, and our support. We can be fair, even when it doesn't benefit us, and we can do the right thing, even when it might make us look like idiots.

We can also take the criticism that is rightfully due, when it comes up. As an employee, I was afraid of Derek's temper and erratic behavior. I didn't feel like he could have a calm discussion about anything, much less about specific concerns that I had with how he was failing our department. My attempt to discuss those concerns with Lucy was an attempt to find someone who could mediate the situation and hopefully speak some sense to the fragility of Derek's ego. I'm not privy to the conversation that Lucy and Derek had after I spoke with her about my concerns, but his reaction leads me to believe that while she may have tried to rectify the situation, she ultimately shirked her responsibility to manage Derek, leaving me to deal with the explosive aftermath. And my fear of his temper was obviously not unfounded as he cornered me in his office and berated me. The stupidity of that whole situation still leaves me feeling frustrated and helpless. As an employee, I didn't know what else I could have done to have avoided such a volatile end result. I felt that it was my right and responsibility to voice my concerns, and even now I don't feel that keeping quiet is the right thing. The only thing that I would have done differently is to have left Lucy out of the whole situation, as her inability to manage more appropriately felt like an absolute betrayal. And it's incredibly difficult to be able to continue a relationship where trust has been broken. And if you give me the option between being berated and betrayed OR just berated, I'll take the latter option any day.

A little (necessary) tangent...

While we're on the subject of betrayal, I want to expand on what this actually can mean to an employee, because on the face of things, you might not even realize that you are doing it. Betrayal is essentially a break in trust and your employees can trust you with a number of different aspects of their jobs, and even their personal lives. An employee can trust you to support their perspective in a discussion where conflict is apparent or trust you to treat them like a human being when they have an emergency. An employee should trust you to be fair when making decisions, or to treat them with the respect that they have diligently earned.

It's not always easy to know the best way to respond to a situation concerning your employees. I will give you some very specific advice and then some very general suggestions. First, do everything you possibly can, so that you do not go back on your word. If you have had a conversation with your employee and discussed your perspective on a certain situation, you should maintain that "stance" and support your employee in future discussions where you may face bureaucratic opposition. I'm not saying that you can't change your mind. But if you do, you should vocalize why your position has changed. Maybe you don't think you owe that to your employee, and from a top heavy perspective, I guess you don't. But if you want to maintain a trust-based relationship with your employee, you should. If you don't, they will feel like you've swiped the rug out from under them, and in the future they will think twice about standing on any rugs when you are around. Which is to say that they won't trust you to back them up or say what needs to be said. They will think that you are spineless, selfish, and just out to protect yourself. Which, if I'm being honest, you are. If you have the cowardice to hide behind your silence or are too insecure to stand up for what you have already said you believe in, then your employees will continue to be disappointed in you. Often, employees will want you to "go to bat" for them, so when you turn on your heel and leave them hanging, you aren't just not going to bat for them, you're stealing their bat and playing for the other side. Don't be that guy, nobody wants that guy on their team.

Like I said, knowing how to respond to a situation concerning your employees can be confusing and the general advice that I would give you is pretty simple in concept, though difficult in implementation. Ask yourself how your employee would want you to respond and if you don't know, then just fucking ask them. Easy right? It's the golden rule, but in a work context, with some swearing and fact checking. I'll give you an example. If your employees want to go grab drinks as a team on a Friday night to let off some steam, what should you do? You like your employees, and really do want to spend time with them in a less regimented setting, but you are unsure of how they will view you after you get a little drunk. So, let's apply the concept. What would your employees want? If they've invited you, they obviously want you to come, but maybe they haven't thought about the alcohol equalizing variable, and you don't know how they might react to your drunken and slurred impromptu decision to break out into a blaze of karaoke glory (I'm not speaking from experience or anything). You don't know how they might react, so just ask them. "Hey team, I'd love to come with you all to get a little tipsy, but I have a tendency to serenade police officers when I've had a little too much to drink. If you were to witness that, will you still respect me when we get back into the office?" (Again not speaking from experience or anything). And you should be able to tell from their responses how they feel. Some may laugh and encourage you to join them, while others may seem to recoil at the thought. In my experience, it depends a lot more on the type of boss you have been up to this point, than it has to do anything with them. Either way, take the feedback to heart and make an appropriate decision.

As a side note, if you know that when you drink alcohol that you always get absolutely shitfaced, (yes that's the professional terminology) then maybe you should do yourself a favor and not have alcohol around your employees. They just might not look at you the same. And also, if you always need to get that drunk, you might have a problem, just saying. Go find yourself a good therapist and get that figured out ASAP. And let's be real, those side notes about serenading police officers after too many cocktails…yeah, that's about me. And I don't always know my limit, so I am super careful about my alcohol intake.

Apologies for the tangent, but it needed to be said. Let's get back into it, shall we?

So, what should Derek have done differently?
I'm going to focus on Derek moving forward because I think we've covered Lucy's areas of improvement quite enough.

When you are in charge of a group of employees, there are bound to be areas where you will disagree on the right way to handle a situation. This can be anything from your employees thinking that you shouldn't scream at your cell phone provider, to your employees not wanting to manage an additional set of responsibilities, to simple disagreements like whether your team should play Whirlyball* or Bowl for the team retreat. Regardless, conflict will forever exist as long as individuals think differently and also have the right to choose. (*If you have never played Whirlyball, do yourself a favor and look it up. It's basically basketball while driving bumper cars using lacross sticks. It's hilarious and SUPER fun even if you are terrible at it.)

Conflict is not innately negative, as some people may assume. It is when people attach strong emotions to conflict that it can become negative. At its base, conflict is a discrepancy between views. If two individuals have different ideas on what they want to eat for lunch, it's considered a conflict. But that doesn't mean that those two people have to get angry at each other and decide to no longer want to be friendly.

Derek definitely needed to have a better understanding of how to manage conflict. But more specifically, he needed to understand how to handle feedback. I believe that conflict and feedback are related because feedback is housed in a difference of opinion. If someone is providing you with constructive criticism, they have a different perspective on the way that you may be handling a certain situation. This is not to say that your way of doing something is right or wrong, it just means that someone else thinks that it could be handled differently.

There are considered to be five types of Conflict Management Styles, including Competing, Collaborating, Compromising, Accommodating, and Avoiding styles* (*Rahim, 2002; Shell, 2001). The Competing style is likely the style that you are most familiar with because it tends to be the loudest. Derek was absolutely an example of someone who used the Competing style, as it is both assertive and uncooperative* (*Unno, 2010). Now, the Competing style, again, is not innately bad. Someone who is using a Competing style is vocal about their perspective but can be inflexible when trying to come to a resolution. This can be appropriate for situations where you are dealing with rules and regulations. If the law says that you cannot break into someone's house, then using a Competing style when dealing with someone who has broken into your house makes a lot of sense right? However, using a Competing style is not always appropriate (obviously). If you were in a different situation, where your employee was attempting to give you feedback for example, using a Competing style would not benefit you, or your employee.

It's no secret that Derek didn't understand how to deal with feedback. When he received my feedback, through Lucy, he could have responded to the situation in a number of ways. If he were to use an Accommodating style, he would have let me know that he understood my concerns and made changes based on my feedback. If he were to have used an Avoiding style, he would have just ignored the feedback altogether and hoped that no one noticed or cared. If he were to use a Collaborating style, he would have tried to figure out a way where we both could have been happy with the situation. And if he were to have used a Compromising style, he would have negotiated an end result that required us both to agree on the best way to proceed, even if it meant that we would both need to "lose" a little of what we wanted from the resolution. While none of these styles is officially the "correct" way to handle a situation, there are surely some styles that seem to make more sense than using a Competing style to badger your employee into submission.

When receiving feedback, it's important to consider that the information you are receiving is as much about you as it is about the person providing the feedback. And in that sense, all feedback is constructive because it provides you with additional information. For example, if you have an employee who tells you that you should stop screaming through the walls of your shared office, it may sound like you need to stop being such a loud piece of shit, but what you should also hear is that your employee is feeling disrespected by your volume, and may even be concerned that you will direct that frustration at them. Regardless, your response should not be to then yell at your employee for their opinion.

What you could do instead is to respond to the feedback through a collaborative discussion where you can both come to an agreement about reasonable changes. Maybe they don't care that you are screaming through the walls, they just don't want you to upset the inevitable consumers (in my case students) who come into the office. Maybe you can both come to an agreement that you are allowed to scream to your hearts content, but only between certain hours of the work day when you know that the office won't be dealing with "customers". Now let's be honest, this is totally bullshit, and you really just shouldn't yell at people like that, but hopefully you get the idea.

Derek was in a league of his own when it comes to the way that he dealt with his frustrations, and while it is important not to stifle those emotions, it is also just as important to manage them appropriately. And it's not an easy task. It is so instinctual to lash out at everyone when you are angry or annoyed by something that has just happened to you. If you think about it, what you are doing is trying to protect yourself from potential threats. It's a trait we've gained through evolution that makes total sense. But it doesn't mean that it's a good way to respond in a professional setting. For example, if your boss has just told you that you aren't performing at the level that they need you to, and that you're now going to have to add additional initiatives to your workload, you have every right to feel frustrated. That doesn't mean that you should then direct that frustration at your employees. And while Derek's frustrations always seemed to be personal, they seemed to result in retaliation against us. As a boss, you have to do better than your initial reactions, and learn to be self-aware. Ask yourself why you are angry, and then channel your energy at the cause of your frustration, instead of at unsuspecting employees who just happen to be in your environment at the time. Be smarter and less of an asshole.

One final thought I will leave you with is the idea of fairness. If you want to be a boss that is respected and appreciated, you have to consider that fairness is about perception. If your employees only have one part of a story, their incomplete view may cause them to view your actions as unfair. Let's go back to the example where Derek handed me an additional campus without sharing the workload. From my perspective, it seemed like I was the only person who was being significantly impacted by the change. Derek was taking on no additional work, and neither was the other Registrar (who I'll remind you was a full two positions higher on the proverbial totem pole). I understood that the Registrar already had a large population, so I was less frustrated that she was not asked to handle the additional students. However, Derek seemed to be spending his time on nothing of consequence. His efforts appeared to be focused on unimportant pieces of the department. It felt like our little row boat was sinking, and while I was bailing water, and figuring out ways to plug up the holes, he was standing up, rocking the boat, and filibustering about the best techniques for manning a yacht. There's a time and place to be loquacious, and neither are on a sinking ship.

It's possible that Derek was actually doing something that was more beneficial than supporting the additional campus. I highly doubt it, but it's possible. If he had, it would have been in his best interest to try to share that information so that he could figuratively tip the scales of "fairness". Let me put it to you this way: If there are four bags of luggage that need to be carried from a car to a hotel room, and there are two bellmen to handle the luggage, it stands to reason that each bellman would handle two of the bags. People tend to get frustrated when they can see a fair division of responsibilities that aren't implemented. Unfairness would be those same four bags of luggage being handled by one bellman while the other bellman was on his cell phone, yelling at his cell phone provider. Now, let's change the scenario a little bit. Let's say that it's the same luggage, and the same bellmen, but while one of the bellmen is handling the luggage, the other is helping a frustrated hotel guest who believes her luggage was misplaced by the hotel staff. The division of responsibilities seems a little more fair, right? While it is not always appropriate to share all of the projects and responsibilities that you may be working on as a boss, it's important to appear fair. Making sure to equally distribute responsibilities can help employees to feel less like they are being overburdened, and more like the team they are part of is handling projects and issues together. They are not a lone slave in ancient Egypt, they are part of a larger construction crew that is working together to build architectural masterpieces.

So...what?: Survival Skills

I'm going to be totally honest and tell you that any advice I'll be providing for dealing with Derek and Lucy is completely based on hindsight. Working for Derek felt claustrophobic and anxiety-ridden. It felt like I was maneuvering a herd of cats through a field of land mines. Every step was bound to be explosive. And for me, that tension built up to a point where I couldn't take it anymore, and I had to leave. And I had no safety net to land on. I didn't have a job to go to, I just knew that staying around any longer would have meant that I would begin to exhibit the worst parts of myself. My sarcastic attitude would no longer be a personality quirk, it would turn into outright indignation coupled with a decline in my work ethic and productivity. So, the advice that I will give you is as follows: Do not let yourself get to this point. Do not let yourself become so frustrated with your boss or even just your job in general that you are ready to leave at a moment's notice. I imagine that most employees are like sticks of dynamite. To a certain extent, most employees start off a new job with a reasonably long fuse. But after every frustrating experience, a little more of that fuse is snipped off, until their fuse is so short that anything will result in detonation. Don't let yourself get to the point where an explosion is inevitable. Now I don't know you, so I can't say how long or short your fuse is, but hopefully you have a good idea. Maybe you are like me, and you don't have that long of a fuse to begin with. If that's the case, start looking for a new job as soon as you start to notice the signs that your boss is an asshole.

They are kind of hard to miss. If you have a longer fuse, feel free to give yourself a little more time to see if your boss can be dealt with. All I am encouraging you to do is to be aware of the situation you are in and react appropriately. Maybe you recognize that your boss is an absolute idiot, but you know that you can put up with that, so you decide to wait for them to be let go. Maybe you see that your boss is just new to management, and you feel like they will likely grow into their position, so you wait for them to get better. My point here is that you need to be responsible for knowing what you will or won't put up with and choose your resulting actions accordingly. I wasn't honest with myself and thought I could put up with Derek's bullshit. And then I found myself feeling righteous and indignant, but also unemployed.

If you are planning to stick around, and again I didn't, so take this with a grain of salt, I feel like you've got three options. You can go on the offensive and try to get your boss fired. You can keep you head down and try not to piss off your boss. Or you can be a kiss-ass and try to stay on your boss's good side. Personally, I'm not cut out for either of the latter. I will warn you that going on the offensive is risky if your company is slow to let people go, because you are setting yourself up to be in a situation that will get much worse before it gets any better. But if you can do it, more power to you. The only advice I have about going on the offensive, is to keep documentation of the frustrating occurrences with date information and as much content as possible. If the occurrences happen in quick succession, then you can provide your information to Human Resources, and hopefully have their support. Like I said, it really depends on the way that your company works, so I don't necessarily recommend this route if you aren't able to handle a tense atmosphere. It's very possible that your company will do nothing to support you, which can be frustrating on its own.

Keeping your head down can look different depending on your industry, and honestly the only way I have been able to do it is to stop caring about the quality and results of my work. And even then, it was really only for a short amount of time. If you were to go this route, you should keep your suggestions to yourself, particularly if you feel that they will cause an adverse reaction from your boss or their constituents. And this works for some people. Some people spend their entire jobs staying in line, which is totally fine and understandable. If keeping a job is more important to you than being happy and productive in your job, then going this route is safe if you are a cog in a much larger machine. Personally, I have never wanted to be a cog. I've always wanted to be the mechanic or the engineer even, so I am not happy keeping my head down. If you are, more power to you.

The last suggestion of kissing-ass isn't a real suggestion. From my perspective, someone who has to bow down to the whims of a dictatorial boss, must not be any good at their job. Don't get me wrong, offering support and helping out when it's needed is not kissing-ass. The people I am referring to are the employees that are terrible at their jobs and must hide their laundry list of weaknesses by overly complimenting their superior. For example, I know of a particularly terrible employee who has no idea how to do his job and relies heavily on an equally unqualified department to support him. But he has done such a "good" job of sucking up that he will never get fired. It won't ever be a consideration until his boss is no longer in charge. And while he rises up the chain of command, his responsibilities are only barely managed (if that) which hurts the rest of the company. By the way, if you're a boss, and you've got someone who is overly eager to pay tribute to you, even if you've just done a mediocre job; you may want to double check to make sure that they don't absolutely suck at their job. It wouldn't hurt to double check that sort of thing.

Ask yourself, do you feel lucky?

Throughout this chapter, we've discussed Lucy, who didn't have the expertise or backbone to give me the support that I needed to thrive. We've also discussed Derek, who was malicious, irrational, and contributed nothing to the team. The following questions are broken into two parts to address the different types of bosses that Lucy and Derek were.

Shitty Boss: Lucy

1. If throughout this chapter you've thought that you may have been like Lucy, where you didn't have the expertise to really support your employees, what have you done to try to overcome that aspect of your skillset? Is it important to you? Why or why not?
2. If you've been in a situation where you could have fought harder to support your employee, can you explain why you didn't? Was it based on your own fear of retaliation? Was it based on concerns about job security? Or did you not agree with your employee's perspective in the first place?
3. Now that you have a little more insight into an employee's perspective on expertise and providing support, is there anything you want to change about your management style?

Shitty Boss: Derek

1. Do you feel like you are quick to get angry? Do you feel like you are unable to contain your frustrated emotions? Do you sometimes direct your anger at someone or something other than the true source of your frustration?
   a. If so, how can you curb your emotions in a way that is not disruptive?
   b. How can you direct your frustrations at the appropriate source?
2. Do you have difficulty responding to feedback?
   a. What about feedback is difficult to hear?

      b. How can you change your perspective on receiving feedback?

      c. What practical steps can you take to improve your ability to take constructive criticism?

3. How do you currently distribute responsibilities amongst your team?

      a. Do you feel that your team believes it to be a fair distribution of tasks? If not, how can you work to improve that?

      b. Do your team's responsibilities appear to be overwhelming and particularly burdensome? Are there any responsibilities that you could assist with?

Now, as an employee, maybe you are at a decision point where you are still trying to figure out what you should do. There might still be some hope that you can get to a point where you are not so frustrated that you are planning to leave your job. You have to ask yourself what is important to you as an employee.

"Asshole" Employee:

1. What do you need to feel satisfied and supported at your job? Does that support need to come from your boss? Can you derive that support from your coworkers, or team?

2. If you feel like you need to be supported by your boss to be satisfied and successful, what makes you feel unsupported?

      a. Can you have a discussion with your boss about your concerns and needs as an employee? Keep in mind that they may not even realize that you feel unsupported. (Yes, some people are that stupid.)

      b. What are your specific grievances? Can you have a discussion with your boss about them? Do you have clear examples?

3. If you haven't had these types of discussions with your boss, how are you contributing to the problem? Even if you don't think so, consider how.
   a. Do you feel like you cannot have this type of discussion with your boss for fear of retaliation? Or are you too hurt, angry, or disappointed to have a rational discussion?
   b. If you could tell your boss how you feel and never have to speak to them again, what would you say? Based on what you would say, how much of that can you change to be constructive criticism?

In the next chapter, we're going to discuss one of the best bosses that I have had the fortune to work for. I truly feel that he has helped me to be a halfway decent boss myself, and I appreciate him immensely for being such a wonderful role model and awesome dude.

CHAPTER 8:
Director Idol

American Idol is one of those reality shows that kind of hurts to watch at the beginning because there are so many terrible singers, and then it slowly evolves into a small group of the talented few who truly have something special. I feel like my professional career, working with all kinds of different management styles and personalities has been similar in the sense that I have had to deal with a good number of frustrating, talentless assholes. However, along the way I have also been fortunate enough to work with really amazing bosses who deserve to make it to the "grand finale". Of all of them, one boss, in particular, has really been outstanding from a practical standpoint. He was everything that I've ever wanted in a boss, and my only real gripe against him is that he ditched me way too soon. Maybe it's because of where I was in my career, or because of my better understanding of my own needs as an employee, but the final boss that I'm going to discuss really continues to stand out in my mind. He's the barometer for which I will compare all future bosses to, and the boss that I strive to be like. I hope to do him justice with this chapter.

We're going to call him Mark, and we're going to play a little catch up here. After leaving FPU, Athena recruited me to work for UB Corp a couple of months later. I wasn't particularly excited to stay in academia, but it was what I knew so I was happy to be getting a paycheck again. Sometime after I started working for UB Corp, Athena got the news that her cancer was back, and she had to again go on an extended medical leave. Eventually, Athena was replaced by a Senior Director, who then hired Mark to manage myself and my coworker. I was wary of new bosses after my experience with Derek, and as I had no part of the hiring process, I was even more scared that our new boss was going to be a total asshole. I remember worrying that he wouldn't understand how our department functioned, or that he would make a lot of changes quickly. And when he started, both of these "worries" actually manifested themselves, but not in the ways that I had imagined.

Our department at UB Corp was responsible for supporting academic record compliance, and we had been functioning as a support team for the Registrar staff at our affiliate schools, like FPU. Unfortunately, with our leadership being absent for some time, we had devolved into a sort of catch all to assist with projects and became more like a "middle man" between affiliate Registrar staff, and the other UB Corp departments. At the time, I liked it because I felt like I was always problem solving and that every day was different.

When Mark started to manage our department, I worried that he would make assumptions about us and then just start to make changes as he saw fit. I was shocked and beyond surprised when he took it upon himself to have one-on-one debriefs with my coworker and I. Remember how I've been telling you in previous chapters that it's important to get a lay of the land before you dive head first into making changes? Yeah, well Mark understood that. He knew that it was important to have a baseline from which to propel himself forward. And not only that, but he actually asked us how we thought the department could improve. And then he worked with us to try to make those changes. Hopefully, you can see why I pretty much love this guy.

Mark understood that we had been a department of two who had sort of fantastical ideas about what we could be, and he also seemed to know how to get us from where we were to where we wanted to be. It was impressive and I still am in awe of the changes that he made. In a short amount of time, Mark was able to shift our department from the reactive position that it was in, to a point where we had a more pivotal role in proactively addressing issues before they became concerns. And he did it with our buy in and full support. He understood where we were coming from, where we wanted to go, and helped us to work as a team to get there. During that time, he also proved his level of expertise and became a force to be reckoned with.

When I say that Mark was a force, you should imagine a bright blue lightsaber, in a battle where right needed to triumph over wrong. Or, where regulations needed to beat out really stupid ideas. Mark was the rock and the hard place that you didn't want to get caught between. He had the documented regulations to support his points, as well as the persuasive agility to overcome the most ridiculous arguments. I still think he's a conversation superhero. But he didn't only use these strengths to protect the laws that our department responsible for upholding, he used them to support our team.

At some point in time, my coworker's job was being evaluated because of a major project that seemed to be continuously failing. Mark knew beyond a shadow of a doubt that the failures were not due to my coworker, and instead were because of insufficient technological resources from our software provider. He fought tirelessly to protect my coworker's job and made sure that evaluations were objective. Needless to say, my coworker kept his position, and with time was able to completely turn the project around.

Later, Mark also fought so that I could get a promotion and a much needed raise. He understood the effort that I had been putting in and valued me as an employee. I didn't have to convince him that I needed a raise, which is astonishing on its own. When I told him that I thought I deserved a raise, he agreed and worked with the budget to get me a significant increase in pay. It was the first time that I had ever felt someone was going to stick their neck out to back me up. He was willing to fight on my behalf so that I could get paid fairly. And if I'm being honest, if he would have gotten me a small increase, it still would have meant a lot. It was the fact that he was willing to be in my corner and go to bat for me without question. I felt valued and respected, and I appreciated that feeling immensely.

Mark also did a great job of treating us like we were more than the jobs that we were paid to do. One of the first questions that Mark asked me when we met was what I saw myself doing in the future. He wanted to know where I planned to be and wanted to help me get there. He's absolutely the reason that I give that advice. It's a holistic perspective that I feel most bosses don't want to address. It's kind of silly, if you think about it. In an age where "millennials" don't take jobs to be career employees, it's a good idea to know what your employee wants to get out of their careers and do your best to provide it to them. When Mark asked me what I wanted to do, I let him know that I eventually wanted to go into some kind of consulting work where I could leverage my knowledge and expertise to support academic institutions. Only a couple of years later, I am doing that in my current position. I didn't even have to leave, and it is largely due to the way that Mark rebranded our department.

While Mark was my boss, I was also working on my dissertation, and he was generously flexible with my time off. He let us know from the beginning that we didn't have to give him advance notice about needing to take time off, and that he was flexible with our schedules as long as we got our work done. It seems like such a small allowance, but for employees who feel regularly stifled by a limited vacation system, Mark's understanding was liberating. Depending on the kind of work that you do, this isn't always possible, obviously. However, when you can make allowances like these it communicates empathy and general human decency.

Mark was also remarkable at training because he was able to simplify difficult topics and make them resonate with his audience. We were quick to recognize Mark's ability to persuade affiliates and other departments to do the right thing but were limited in our own understanding of the regulations and experience with overcoming conflicts. Mark was happy to schedule team summits where we would all come together so that he could share his expertise and train us on his particular set of skills. I felt like I learned more working for Mark in a year than I had in the entirety of my academic programs, which is both amazing and embarrassing.

Mark also felt that it was important to be honest, as a sign of respect. And he would share as much information as he could with us so that we never felt blindsided by the many changes that were bound to occur. I appreciated that he wanted to know our perspective on different topics and wasn't threatened by the amount of tribal knowledge that I already held concerning our affiliates. He understood that we were a team with combined strengths and weaknesses, and he never held either against us.

When I think about it now, Mark could have very easily tried to keep me from advancement. He could have muted my strengths, but instead he understood that my knowledge and experience contributed to the team's strength overall. He was secure in his expertise and didn't need to trample all over me to console his ego.

One of the last things that I will mention about Mark, is by far one of the things that I appreciated most about him as a boss: Mark made it a point to have fun. That doesn't mean that we didn't work hard, we absolutely did. What I mean to say is that Mark worked diligently to make sure our team environment was based on camaraderie. Our weekly team check-ins started off with catching up on personal updates in addition to our work updates. And our team retreats included team dinners and team building activities like bowling (and beer). This perpetuated the idea that Mark cared about us as people. Not only did he care about our professional goals and career aspirations, but he also cared about making sure that we liked working with each other. In previous jobs, this had always kind of happened organically. Because we were a remote team, Mark made sure to make it a focal point. And it is something that I plan to continue.

So, what did Mark do right?

Mark will probably always be the boss that I aspire to be like. He cared about us as individuals, he protected us and fought for us, and he is one of the smartest guys that I know. These are all pretty easy things that you can do as a boss, except maybe the last part. I mean it's easy to care about how your employee's day is going. Even from a "bottom line" perspective, if your employee is having a shitty day, anything you can do to help with turning that around will likely improve their mood and subsequently their efficiency and productivity. Makes sense to care about your employees, right?

Protecting your employees and speaking on their behalf may be a little more difficult, because you may have to deal with the "attacks" that would otherwise be directed at them. But again, if you think about it from a "bottom line" perspective, it's cheaper to fight to protect and support your employees if it means that you will retain them. The cost of turnover, especially high levels of it, can be astronomical and for the most part avoidable. You can literally save your department (and company) thousands of dollars, if you are willing to get yelled at to shield your employees, just suck it up. The good employees are totally worth it.

When I say that Mark is one of the smartest guys I know, I mean that he is all around intelligent with book smarts and street smarts. You don't have to be as awesome as Mark, but you should be smart enough to earn the respect of your employees. Or, you should be smart enough to know when your employees are smarter than you and then be okay with that. And it's more important that your employees respect you for your knowledge and experience than it is for them to actually think that you are smarter than them. Honestly a good boss is one who can be the smartest person at the table, but also doesn't have to be.

Mark also instituted some really simple and awesome strategies that pretty much anyone can do. Every week, we met as a team to update each other on the progress of our different projects and then had separate one-on-one meetings to discuss any areas where we might need additional guidance or had more updates. Seriously, make a recurring meeting invite, and just start having an informal conversation. This relaxed environment serves the purpose of regular communication, while also normalizing opportunities for feedback. And most of the time, these meetings are something that you'll look forward to because you will grow to like speaking with your employees more than anyone else. Because we were a remote team, Mark also made sure that we met in person at least once or twice a year so that we could spend time together and get the chance to have a good time. Keeping a remote team like ours engaged is no small success, but I believe that Mark was able to manage us with modest but powerful methods.

Did it work?

Mark's management style was absolutely what our team needed. He was the backbone of our department, and his initiative to rebrand us truly shifted the way that we were able to enact significant improvements. He also did a great job of supporting us in a way that helped with retention.

As I said, while I was working for Mark, I was also finishing up my doctorate. My goal was to move on once I had finished school to something that I felt was more along the lines of my intended career path. Working for Mark totally changed my perspective on leaving the company. I was no longer set on making a change and was honestly excited to stick around to see how the department would grow and evolve. I could tell that Mark was going to drive us toward a more sustainable position, and I was happy to be along for the ride.

I think it is safe to say that Mark made significantly beneficial changes to our department in less than a year. He was able to take a floundering department with lots of potential and help us to become a flourishing team that operated on a sustainable and proactive level. I just wish he wouldn't have left so soon.

What Next?

Instead of asking you what you think Mark would have done in some made up scenarios, the next couple of questions are set up to give you the time to reflect on what you can do next? It is my strong opinion that Mark was an awesome boss, and hopefully you agree. And while it may be difficult to measure up, I think it's important that we continuously strive to be better than we are.

1. Now that you've had a chance to read about how awesome Mark is, what were some of the qualities or strategies that he used that really stood out to you?
    a. How can you try to embody these qualities?
    b. How can you utilize these strategies to your advantage?
2. If you feel that you are at Mark's level of awesomeness, be honest with yourself and consider what your employees think of you.
    a. Do your employees feel the same? Why or why not?
    b. If you don't know, how can you find out?
3. Is there anything that you do that your employees appreciate that wasn't discussed?
    a. Why do your employees appreciate you?

b. How can you make that sustainable?

4. What else can you do? How can you continue to succeed, as there is always room for improvement?

Final Thoughts

As we come to the end of the final chapter on my experience with different types of bosses, I hope you've got a pretty good understanding of how you fit into the whole picture. Whether you are a boss, or an employee, you play a role in the situation and may unknowingly contribute to a negative outcome. Even though Mark was an amazing boss, like any other human, he had his own faults just like the rest of us. It's important to be self-aware and recognize what those areas of improvement are, and to keep working to be better.

The last chapter of this experiment is my least favorite, because I'm hoping to give you a little insight into my current experience of being a boss. I plan to share some perspective from my team who I have not encouraged or bribed in any way. (Okay, maybe I took them out for drinks and am blackmailing them with karaoke videos...kidding...I deleted those.) I think it's only fair to share my own experience as I have thoroughly shit-talked a bunch a lot of my previous supervisors.

CHAPTER 9:
In All Fairness...A Cynical Conclusion

I'm writing this chapter because I don't think it's fair to heavily judge a bunch of other people without also shining that interrogative spotlight on my own flaws. I'll do my best to evaluate myself with the help of the perspectives of the wonderful and amazing people that work on my team. But first, just a little bit of additional background on how I stepped into my role.

We've talked about Mark, and how he was an awesome boss. Well, unfortunately, Mark decided to abandon our team after about a year and a half of working with us. This is absolutely a complaint because I miss him terribly. He was an amazing guy to work for and I still strive to be able to measure up.

When Mark let me know that he was leaving, I promptly let him know that I did not want to take his place. In our small department of four, other than Mark, I was the only other person who had any sort of lead role, and knowing the culture of our company, I knew that they would likely try to get me to take the job. I had loads of concerns about the feasibility of being able to fill Mark's shoes. I didn't have his years of experience or level of expertise. And I definitely didn't have the strong reputation that Mark had built for himself. I was working on my doctorate at the time, and just wanted to finish school. Mark let me know that he would pass the information along, but that he was surprised that I wasn't jumping at the chance.

A couple of days later, a C-level type contacted me and tried to convince me to take the job. I let her know that I would think about it, but that I still wasn't convinced that I was the right person for the job. I didn't want my coworkers (who would become my employees) to be frustrated with the change. So, I had a chat with them. Both of them were surprised that I wasn't planning to step into Mark's role, and actually seemed pretty adamant that I take the promotion. I was touched and equally surprised that they felt so strongly about it. With their support, some very aggressive prodding from the top, and Mark's blessing, I accepted the promotion, and that's pretty much how I ended up here. I worked my way into the role, and while I am extremely biased, I am happy to have hit all the rungs on the ladder on my way up.

As a director, I have done my best to give my employees the same structure and support that Mark put in place. I'm sure that I haven't done as well of a job, but hopefully they appreciate the effort. Some of the things that I've continued to do include the weekly team meetings and weekly one on one check ins. I felt that these were so important when Mark was around and don't want to lose the value of team communication and insight. I've also kept up the team retreats where we meet in person at least twice a year. As we are a team that works remotely, I feel that it is still majorly important to get in-person face to face time, and have worked to make our time together educational, productive, and fun.

In addition to the more pragmatic things, I have also done my best to be honest, fair, respectful, trusting, and trustworthy. I share the information that I have when it is appropriate and effects them, and I also share my feelings, both the positive and negative, about the different projects that we work with. I try to be fair when I am delegating out projects or dividing up responsibilities. I think it's important to do my share, and make sure to support my team as they need me to. In this way, I feel that I am also being respectful of their time. Trust is also a gigantic foundational piece of what makes our team work. We all trust each other to work hard, chip-in, and do an amazing job. In my opinion, this is no small feat due to the reality of what it's like to work remotely. I can't just pop over to someone's desk and make sure that they are working hard or working at all. But it's also wonderful to know that even though I can't do that, I really don't have to. I feel that giving my team the flexibility and autonomy to get their jobs done has made them more comfortable and actually more hardworking, if that's even possible.

Taking a page out of Mark's book, I've also tried to work with my employees to figure out what's important to them in a job, and a boss. During our weekly check-ins, we spend time discussing work-related items and non-work-related items. This has been anything from providing perspective on their dissertation, to listening to great television show ideas, to chatting about home renovations and Lego messes. Because of this, they are some of my favorite people in the world. But I also have tried to use this to understand what they want to do in their roles and provide them with the project opportunities to expand their skillsets. I believe this also shows them that I am willing and able to listen and respond to their feedback. That being said, I actually asked them for some of their feedback on what they think of me as a boss, and they were pretty honest.

I asked them questions regarding areas where I can improve and what my strengths are and kept their identities anonymous in order to limit any concerns that they might have about retaliation. I truly appreciate their ability to share their honest perspective and hope to improve in the areas that they have suggested.

In response to providing feedback on areas where I can improve, one employee states, "There is a balance that needs to be struck between autonomy and supervision, and while close, Crystal is a bit too far on the autonomy side...Something along the lines of setting up hard deadlines for aspects of projects...That kind of extra attention would take her to the next level." It's great to hear that I am at the very least not someone who micromanages others, but that I can stand to provide a little more oversight. This is helpful to know that it is something my team may need to remain on task and feel that they have met their responsibilities.

Another employee suggests that I could "delegate responsibility a little more often." The employee continues, "Crystal is smart and hardworking and can usually do a task quicker than if she were to explain it to others, but sharing responsibilities can make a team feel more included." This is actually feedback that I have received before and have been working on, so it's good to know that it's still an area to expand on. I definitely took on some of Athena's management style and am realizing that taking the extra time to show an employee how to do something is both good for cross-training and for team inclusion. In explanation of myself, I honestly am so used to working with slackers that it's weird to work with a group of people that want to work hard. Weirdos.

Another employee's gripe was that we don't spend enough time together in person. While they note that it's based on budgetary constraints, it is a totally valid concern, and it helps me to know what is important to them. While working remotely allows for a lot more flexibility, it can also feel isolating and nerve-wracking. If being in-person can solve for that, I should do what I can to make that happen. Hope they are prepared for way more, weird face time with me and random lunch invites when I am in their neighborhoods. It's helpful to know that my introversion is showing.

Phew...I thought that was going to be a lot worse than it was. Okay, moving on to the strengths, because they apparently seem to think that I have some.

To start, one employee responded, "I love and appreciate how trusting she is...I never fear retaliation when a necessary venting session occurs...Her constant communication and attention to the needs of her team are effective and keep everyone on task." Another says, "Crystal is good at empowering employees and giving them the freedom they need to complete and manage projects without getting bogged down with micromanaging...[She] is also very good at providing support when requested." And finally, "[she is] smart, hardworking, understanding, allows people to be themselves...gives praise, and doesn't ask team members to do anything that she would not do herself." While the areas of improvement are a good gauge of what I can do better, it's great to know that I am succeeding in the areas where I have put my focus such as being trusting and respectful. It is also particularly touching to know that they recognize that I would not ask them to do something that I wouldn't do. I believe it's only fair, and it is a point of pride for me.

Okay, hopefully this gives you some additional insight into the perspective that I come from as an employee and as a boss. I believe that there is always room for improvement, regardless of your career progression. It's important to ask for feedback so that you know which areas to focus on, and to understand how you are affecting others.

In truth, if you are for some reason, still reading this book, the odds are that you are neither a Shitty Boss or an Asshole Employee, and you are just trying to figure out how to deal with the stress of work. Maybe you thought that you were a Shitty Boss. Take solace in the thought that if you are reading this book, you at least have the self-awareness to know that you have room for improvement. Maybe you have a Shitty Boss, and now understand that you might be contributing to the problems. Either way, I hope you know that this isn't meant to be a self-help book that tells you how to be a better anything. But, if you've learned something along the way, then I guess that's pretty awesome.

If not, and you're a list type of person, I'll leave you with a list of bullet points as a cheat sheet reminder for things to focus on if you want to be a good boss. This is advice that I try to follow, myself, and it seems to be working out pretty well.

Anyway, thanks for taking the time to dig through the bullshit. Hopefully you've read something that resonates with you. If not, no refunds, sorry. Make it a great one!

"Don't Be A Shitty Boss" Cheat Sheet (in no particular order)

- **RESPECT:** Treat your employees the way that you would want to be treated. You should not have an unearned, overbearing ego around them. You are part of a team. You need to LEAD AND FOLLOW. And FORGET ABOUT MICROMANAGING them.
- **TRUST**: Earn as much trust as possible by respecting them and trusting them first. You can also do this by providing good and ethical explanations for your actions. Another really common sense way to do this is to DO WHAT YOU SAY YOU ARE GOING TO DO.
- **COMMUNICATION:** You should regularly communicate with your employees and BE FUCKING HONEST! It also helps to learn how to "translate" the different languages that will exist between departments, employees, and supervisors. Learn to read between the lines and figure out what everyone is trying to accomplish so that you can GET SHIT DONE.
- **COMPETENCE:** Understand the roles of your employees and know how to support them. The more you know about their responsibilities, the more you can speak intelligently about them when needed. And along these lines, also be willing to admit when they are smarter than you, because they already know it and will respect you more when you admit it. From a practical perspective, it's also important to be the "COG AND THE ENGINEER". You should be able to do the job itself, but also understand how it fits into the bigger picture.
- **PROTECTION:** Be a force field that surrounds your employees. Back them up, even if they are wrong, and coach them privately. DON'T BE AN ASSHOLE, even if they

sometimes deserve it. And fight for them, for what is right and what is fair. As a side note, swear around them when you are mad at other people, but don't swear at them. And make the tough calls so that they don't have to.

- **DELEGATION:** Balancing responsibilities out amongst team members, including yourself can be difficult but supports cross-training and team inclusion. Don't be afraid to get in the trenches with your employees and work alongside them. Big projects should be considered team efforts, even if they "belong" to one or a few employees. But also be able to let them take ownership of projects. YOU DON'T HAVE TO DO EVERYTHING.

- **CROSS-TRAINING AND CONTINGENCY PLANS:** Have contingency plans so that you know how you are going to handle something when an employee is out or inevitably leaves. Do this by cross-training as much as possible.

- **COACH AND REWARD:** Respond to their actions appropriately. Appreciate good behavior and award them for taking initiative. And when they fuck up, DON'T BERATE THEM. Use their error as a learning experience to recognize similar situations in the future and do better next time.

- **CARE ABOUT YOUR EMPLOYEES:** Know who they are inside and outside of the job. Ask about their weekends, their families, their pets, their hobbies...GIVE THEM WEIRD NICKNAMES, create an environment where inside jokes are common and you laugh with each other.

- **PROPEL THEM FORWARD:** Understand that they may not want this job forever, and help them get to their next step, even if it means that they are leaving you. If they are sticking around, give them as many opportunities to move up as possible. And along those lines, you should give them the opportunities to excel instead of making them do things they don't want to do. When you get a shitty employee, you should coach, train, and document as much as you can. Figure out how to help them to improve so that you can retain them or help them to move on to what they actually want to be doing. And if they aren't shitty, but just want some extra experience, GIVE THEM THE OPPORTUNITY TO SUCCEED.

- **GET FEEDBACK:** Ask for their feedback and do your best to HANDLE IT MATURELY. And if you aren't sure if they'll answer you honestly, let them provide anonymous feedback. Give them a safe way to help you. Because whether you realize it or not, whatever they say should help you. It also helps to ask someone outside of your team, who will be honest with you, how you can improve. Significant others don't count.

- **BE A ROLE MODEL:** Be the person that they respect, that they trust. Be the person they laugh with and vent to. BE THE BOSS THAT DESERVES TO HAVE THEM ON YOUR TEAM. If you are grateful for them, they just might be grateful for you.

ACKNOWLEDGEMENTS

In order of "appearance" (sort of)...first of all, thank you to Tim Leslie for being a super awesome roommate who reminded me about National Novel Writing Month (NaNoWriMo), which is the entire month of November where crazy people like us decide to hunker down and write a novel. Thanks also for being you! Knowing you did this regularly encouraged me to believe that I could.

To Brian Luhmann, Psy.D. for helping me come up with the most cathartic and hilarious book topic ever, I love you so much that I could marry you. Which is to say that I did, because you are my lobster and are destined to put up with my crazy project ideas for the rest of our lives. Thanks for being the first to read this, in it's weirdest format. Thank you also for dealing with my anxieties about releasing this, for loving me when I don't love myself, and for just being the all-around raddest dude that I know.

To Daniel Esquivel, Alex Alt, and Emily Carpenter, I cannot thank you enough for suffering through the first rounds of edits. Your perspective and encouragement are worth so much to me. I truly would not have felt ready to let this out into the world without any of you.

To Bryan Irzyk for being an awesome coworker and even better friend. Thanks for writing the foreword. It's full of lies but I thank you for them anyway. Thanks for the weird nicknames!

To all of the bosses that I've had, awesome and not-so-awesome, thank you for the experience. Thank you for the stories. For the not-so-awesome bosses, I hope you know that by now I only appreciate the lessons you've taught me. If for some reason you are reading this, I hope you can learn some lessons of your own. And for the awesome bosses, thank you for being the amazing role models that I needed and continue to look up to. I hope to follow the path you've laid out for me.

To my friends who have always supported my crazy ideas and not thought too hard about it when I disappeared from social obligations; thank you for letting me hibernate and for still being friends with me when I ventured back into the wild. To my family, hopefully I didn't embarrass you too much. Thanks for loving me anyway.

To Sara Bareilles for music magic while I wrote; to Netflix for necessary background noise while I wrote at 2 a.m. (because that's when my brain works); and to Disaronno and Dr. Pepper for giving me the liquid courage to get out of my own way...thanks a billion.

And to anyone else who's reading this, thanks for taking the time, truly. I don't know what possessed you to read this, but I hope you got something worthwhile out of it.

-Dirt Out

ABOUT THE AUTHOR

Crystal Ishihara, Ph.D. considers herself to be an aging millennial who knows things about Disney, Star Wars, and crazy craft ideas. She earned her Doctorate of Philosophy in Business Psychology and currently works in records compliance while also being an adjunct professor on the weekends. Originally from Aiea, Hawaii, she is a Southern California transplant who loves colorful tattoos, swearing, and traveling everywhere. If she could have a superpower, she would want to transport anywhere instantaneously because that L.A. traffic is no joke, and six hour flights to Hawaii feel like forever. She was technically a child of the 90's, but doesn't remember most of it as a recent trivia-night with her team proved. She loves doing escape rooms, and has ALWAYS escaped. She even started a consulting business to support escape rooms, just so that she could do more of them. You can visit www.ishihumann.com (shameless plug) to learn more!

Ok, that's it. Why are you still here?

Seriously...this isn't a Marvel movie.

Made in the USA
San Bernardino, CA
16 September 2019